# 31 Days Of Vanity

DEVOTIONS FROM ECCLESIASTES

Dr. Mike Smith

Franklin Publishing
PRINCETON, TEXAS

Copyright © 2020 by Mike Smith.

All rights reserved. No part of this publication may be reproduced, distributed or transmitted in any form or by any means, including photocopying, recording, or other electronic or mechanical methods, without the prior written permission of the publisher, except in the case of brief quotations embodied in critical reviews and certain other noncommercial uses permitted by copyright law. For permission requests, write to the publisher, addressed "Attention: Permissions Coordinator," at the address below.

Kelly Carr / Franklin Publishing
1215 Juniper
Princeton, Texas 75407

www.FranklinPublishing.org

Ordering Information:

Quantity sales. Special discounts are available on quantity purchases by corporations, associations, and others. For details, contact the "Special Sales Department" at the address above.

Except where otherwise indicated, all Scripture quotations are taken from the New King James Version®. Copyright © 1982 by Thomas Nelson. Used by permission. All rights reserved.

31 Days Of Vanity: Devotions From Ecclesiastes / Mike Smith. —1st ed.

ISBN-13: 978-1-7320028-7-6
ISBN-10: 1-7320028-7-8

# Contents

Introduction to Ecclesiastes ............................ 9
Day 1 ............................................................... 11
Day 2 ............................................................... 16
Day 3  Wisdom ............................................... 19
Day 4  Wit ....................................................... 23
Day 5  Wine .................................................... 26
Day 6  Women ................................................ 29
Day 7  Wealth ................................................. 32
Day 8  Work .................................................... 35
Day 9  Worship .............................................. 40
Day 10  Watch ................................................ 44
Day 11  Without a Mate ................................ 48
Day 12  World of Politics ............................. 52
Day 13  Worship Without Jesus .................. 55
Day 14  Wicked Politicians .......................... 58
Day 15  Wealth Cannot Satisfy .................... 62
Day 16  Wealth Cannot Give Security ........ 65
Day 17  Wish I Had Never Been Born ........ 68
Day 18  Worthy Name ................................... 72
Day 19  Why So Much Evil .......................... 77

Day 20  Without Breath ............................................. 82
Day 21  World of Surprises ...................................... 87
Day 22  World Leaders ............................................. 91
Day 23  Warnings to Workers ................................. 95
Day 24  Wagging Tongues ........................................ 99
Day 25  Washington ................................................ 102
Day 26  What Is Life About? ................................. 107
Day 27  What a Song .............................................. 111
Day 28  What a Senior Citizen ............................. 114
Day 29  What a School ........................................... 118
Day 30  What a Stewardship ................................ 121
Day 31  Wise Summary ......................................... 124
    Bibliography ..................................................... 127
    About the Author ............................................ 129

## *Dedication*

I dedicate this book to my four grandsons. They have brought so much joy to my life. They have cost me financially but it has been worth every penny. William James Gardner was born

September 18, 1998. He was born with a clef lip but the family felt he was just right. The surgery to correct the lip at his early age was very tense for me. I wanted to ease the pain from my daughter but I felt so helpless. As a young boy, as soon as he would arrive at my house for a visit he would reach out his hand to walk around the block. What memories! On one occasion upon our return from going around the block, he wanted to get into the birdbath. As Paw Paw I have rarely denied my grandsons requests. I lifted him up and into the birdbath. He thought it was great but the rest of the family had other feelings. He has remained active in church and presently is in college preparing to work in church media.

Logan Curtis Smith was born January 9, 2004. He has always been a clean orderly young man. He and his brother worked for the college this past summer. It was good to see how hard they worked.

Jacob Gardner was born 05-05-05. He is the comic of the family. He is also the Trump supporter and politician. He likes serious discussions. I enjoy sharing our family history with him. He probably will be the only one to remember our heritage or value all the old pictures I have collected.

Landon Cole Smith was born November 9, 2006. Landon loves sports and fishing. He also will share a corny joke. He asked me, "Did you hear about the kidnapping at school?" I said "no." His response was, "He woke up."

Landon and Logan both played linebacker on their football teams. Logan knew exactly where to line up and how to read the offense, but could have been more aggressive. Landon had no clue where he was supposed to line up. However, when the ball was snapped Landon was first to tackle the runner. Both play baseball and have many medals.

Every year I take all four on a Paw Paw trip. We went fishing with a guide and had a blast. We have been to baseball card shows. We've been on long train rides with one having a wreck. We've been to several pro baseball games. We've been to the Hall of Fame pro football game in Canton, Ohio. We've been to see Baylor play in bowl games. We stay in nice hotels and eat anywhere the boys want to eat. I do not require baths or brushing of teeth or how long or if they sleep. We have many good memories. Solomon made many mistakes in his pursuits in Ecclesiastes. I know boys will be boys and my grandsons may pursue some of the ways of the world. I pray they will quickly see like Solomon all is vanity except Jesus.

²⁹ *And God gave Solomon wisdom and exceedingly great understanding, and largeness of heart like the sand on the seashore.*
³⁰ *Thus Solomon's wisdom excelled the wisdom of all the men of the East and all the wisdom of Egypt.*
³⁴ *And men of all nations, from all the kings of the earth who had heard of his wisdom, came to hear the wisdom of Solomon.*

—1 KINGS 4:29-30, 34

# Introduction to Ecclesiastes

The 39 books of the Old Testament can be divided into five categories:
- LAW (5)
- HISTORY (12)
- WISDOM (5)
- MAJOR PROPHETS (5)
- MINOR PROPHETS (12)

The wisdom books have always fascinated me. I have many unanswered questions when I read them. But my heart is also warmed to God by the poetic language. I have previously written devotional books from Proverbs and Psalms. This devotional book from Ecclesiastes is my third devotional book.

The format for these daily thoughts are:
1. Read the manuscript
2. Review the material
3. Remember your maker
4. Roar with mirth
5. Reflect on the message

# Day 1

## READ THE MANUSCRIPT

Ecclesiastes 1:1, "The words of the Preacher, the son of David, king in Jerusalem."

## RECEIVE THE MATERIAL

- I am a firm believer that before you study a passage in the Bible you review or acquaint yourself with the background material of the biblical book from which you are reading. In this case what is the background of Ecclesiastes?

- I required my students in the Survey of the Old Testament class to learn five things about every book in the Old Testament. The final exam for the course was to list the Who, What, When, Where, and Why of every book in the Old Testament. It would do us well to review these basic questions for Ecclesiastes.

*WHO? Who wrote Ecclesiastes?*

- SOLOMON

- Critical scholars have and will continue to debate the authorship of Ecclesiastes. I agree a close examination will leave one asking questions. But a reading of Ecclesiastes 1:1: "The words of the preacher, the son of David, king in Jerusalem," who else could this be other than Solomon?

**WHAT?** *What division of the Bible is Ecclesiastes?*

- WISDOM
- The Hebrew title is Qoheleth which is a rare term, found only in Ecclesiastes. It comes from the word Qahal meaning to call for an assembly. It describes one who addresses an assembly. Thus, Ecclesiastes means Preacher. The title is actually from Green word ekklesia from which we get our word church. 1

**WHEN?** *When did Solomon write Ecclesiastes?*

- 900 B. C.
- Solomon wrote the Song of Solomon as a young man in 970 B. C.
- Solomon wrote Proverbs as a middle-aged man in 950 B. C.
- Solomon wrote Ecclesiastes as an old man in 900 B. C.

**WHERE?** *From where did he write the book?*

- JERUSALEM
- Ecclesiastes 1:12, "I, the preacher, was king over Israel in Jerusalem..."

**WHY?** *Why did he write Ecclesiastes?*

- VANITY
- The key verse is Ecclesiastes 1:2, "Vanity of vanities, saith the preacher, vanity of vanities, all is vanity."

- Vanity is used 38 times in Ecclesiastes. The word hebel means emptiness, futile, vapor, that which vanishes quickly and leaves nothing behind. 2

- Solomon depicts life as meaningless. Solomon is a pessimist. Contrast to Jesus who says in John 10:10, "I am come that they might have life, and that they might have it more abundantly."

- The purpose of the book is to show that a life without God is useless. Throughout the book, Solomon tries a number of pursuits to find meaning in life, only to reflect that "all is vanity."

- Every believer needs a Biblical worldview. What does the Bible say? Ecclesiastes asks and answers the question, "Is life worth living?"

- The book primarily covers seven subjects:
    1. Time – 1:1-11; 3:1-15
    2. Wisdom – 1:12-18, 2:12-17, 6:10-7:4, 7:7-29
    3. Wealth – 2:1-11, 2:18-26, 4:4-8, 5:10-6:6, 11:1-6
    4. Politics – 3:15-17, 4:1-3, 4:13-16, 5:8-9, 8:2-6, 9:3-10:17
    5. Death – 3:18-22, 9:3-10, 11:7-12:7
    6. Friendship – 4:9-12
    7. Religion – 5:1-7, 8:9-9:1

Another outline of the book when asking the question "Is life worth living?" is:
1. The problem – Chapters 1-10
2. The answer – Chapters 11-12

Solomon searched for meaning in life by pursing:
1. Wisdom – 1:17-18
2. Wit – 2:1-2
3. Wins – 2:3
4. Women – 2:7

5. Wealth – 2:8
  6. Work – 2:19

After all these pursuits he declared "all is vanity", useless, meaningless, empty.

## SUICIDE

Suicide is on the rise in the United States. Since 1999 the rate has increased approximately 30%. In 2016, 45,000 Americans took their own life. There are a number of contributing factors, such as:

  1. Relationship problems
  2. Financial troubles
  3. Mental health issues[3]

Help exists: Suicide Hotline – 1-800-273-8255 and Kids Help 1-800-668-6868.

Ecclesiastes is a story of a man who tried it all and found it meaningless. At the end of Ecclesiastes in Chapter 12:13-14, he concludes that life does have meaning if you fear God and forget not his commandments. Jesus is the answer.

## REMEMBER YOUR MAKER

Lord, thank you for giving me life and abundant life.

## ROAR WITH MIRTH

Johnny's mother looked out the window and noticed him "playing church" with their cat. He had the cat sitting quietly and he was preaching to it. She smiled and went about her work. A while later she heard loud meowing and hissing and rant back to the open window to see Johnny baptizing the cat in a tub of water. She called out, "Johnny, stop that! The cat is afraid of water!" Johnny looked up at her and said, "He should have thought about that before he joined my church!"

## REFLECT ON THE MESSAGE

Life is worth living with Jesus.

# Notes

[1] Wilkinson & Boa, p. 169
[2] Wiersbe, p. 15
[3] Psychology today.com, April 29, 210 article by Dr. Alex Lickerman, The Six Reasons People Attempt Suicide

# Day 2

## READ THE MANUSCRIPT

Ecclesiastes 1:1-11, "The words of the Preacher, the son of David, king in Jerusalem. Vanity of vanities, saith the Preacher, vanity of vanities; all is vanity. What profit hath a man of all his labour which he taketh under the sun? One generation passeth away, and another generation cometh: but the earth abideth forever. The sun also ariseth, and the sun goeth down, and hasteth to his place where he arose. The wind goeth toward the south, and turneth about unto the north; it whirleth about continually, and the wind returneth again according to his circuits. All the rivers run into the sea; yet the sea is not full; unto the place from whence the rivers come, thither they return again. All things are full of labour; man cannot utter it: the eye is not satisfied with seeing, nor the ear filled with hearing. The thing that hath been, it is that which shall be; and that which is done is that which shall be done: and there is no new thing under the sun. Is there anything whereof it may be said, See, this is new? it hath been already of old time, which was before us. There is no remembrance of former things; neither shall there be any remembrance of things that are to come with those that shall come after."

## RECEIVE THE MATERIAL

CHANGE

Have you ever heard the expression "the more things change the more they stay the same?" Solomon presents a "cyclical" view of life. He is amazed how generations of people come and go, yet things of this world stay the same. Solomon uses nature to say that nothing really changes (1:4-7).

1. Earth – 1:4
2. Sun – 1:5
3. Wind - 1:6
4. Sea – 1:7

Solomon then concludes that nothing is really new (1:8-11). Man seeks for something new (v. 8). Why? They are not satisfied. Let a new restaurant open in town. There is a line and waiting list for the first month. After the newness wears off, you can find a seat there anytime. People are attracted to something. Ecclesiastes 1:9 is an often-quoted verse: "There is nothing new under the sun."

How can this be true? We constantly are seeing changes and new things in our world. From the five-party telephone line, to transcontinental cables, to cell phones, to phones/computers you wear on your wrist.

Solomon is not saying new things are not created. Just the opposite. Solomon is rich enough to have every new toy made in his day. He is expressing frustration of how acquiring new things does not change the old discontentment he has. The multiple new things, be it restaurants, electronics, or amusement parks, will not meet the fundamental need of man found only in a relationship with God through his son, Jesus Christ.

Lanny Wolfe wrote in *Only Jesus Can Satisfy Your Soul*, "The world will try to satisfy that longing in your soul. You may search the wide world over, but you will be just as before. You'll never find true satisfaction until you've found the Lord. For only Jesus can satisfy your soul." [1]

## REMEMBER YOUR MAKER

God, thank you for satisfying my need. You are sufficient.

## ROAR WITH MIRTH

The frugal man walked into the house panting and almost completely exhausted. "What happened, Honey?" asked his wife. "It's a great new idea I have," he gasped. "I ran all the way home behind the bus and saved $1.50." "That wasn't too smart," replied his wife. "Why didn't you run behind a taxi and save $10?"

## REFLECT ON THE MESSAGE

There is nothing new under the sun.

# Notes

[1] Hughesnews.com

# Day 3

# Wisdom

**READ THE MANUSCRIPT**

Ecclesiastes 1:12-18, "I the Preacher was king over Israel in Jerusalem. And I gave my heart to seek and search out by wisdom concerning all things that are done under heaven: this sore travail hath God given to the sons of man to be exercised therewith. I have seen all the works that are done under the sun; and, behold, all is vanity and vexation of spirit. That which is crooked cannot be made straight: and that which is wanting cannot be numbered. I communed with mine own heart, saying, Lo, I am come to great estate, and have gotten more wisdom than all they that have been before me in Jerusalem: yea, my heart had great experience of wisdom and knowledge. And I gave my heart to know wisdom, and to know madness and folly: I perceived that this also is vexation of spirit. For in much wisdom is much grief: and he that increaseth knowledge increaseth sorrow."

## REVIEW THE MATERIAL

The King James Version begins verse 12 as "I the preacher". The New International Version says, "I the Teacher...," and the Good News Translation says, "I the Philosopher..." Why the different descriptions? The Hebrew word is *Qoheleth* and it is difficult to translate. Solomon was king but he also spoke before the people as a preacher would. He would also write as a teacher. His words would sound like a philosopher. Solomon, the same man, spoke in different roles. [1]

In Ecclesiastes 1:12-18, Solomon describes himself as a philosopher in search for the meaning of life. These verses describe Solomon's pursuit in wisdom and education. Philosophers then and now hold that the pursuit of wisdom is the highest calling.

From Plato to present day, philosophers ask questions in pursuit to the meaning of life. [2]

In Verse 13, he describes this pursuit as <u>work</u>. Solomon says it is a grievous task. Life is tough and it is a grind. The questions of life are difficult. It takes concentrated effort to find the answers.

In Verse 14, Solomon describes this pursuit as <u>worthless</u>. Solomon says he has seen all the works, the pursuits of life, and all are meaningless and for man to pursue them is like grasping at the wind. The workaholic and alcoholic are the opposite in their efforts. One gives himself to the things of life and one tries to escape life. Both come up empty. In Verse 1:15 he describes this pursuit as <u>wasteful</u>. Solomon is saying we cannot change the past, so why worry over it. Man cannot fix all of life's problems.

In verses 1:16-18, he describes this pursuit of <u>wisdom</u>. The pursuit of wisdom did not give Solomon the answers he was looking for. In fact, it only resulted in more problems and questions. To think that wisdom or knowledge will satisfy you is a myth. For every answer, educators will tell you the more you know, the more you know you don't know.

In the Garden of Eden in Genesis, Satan offered to Eve the fruit that would give her knowledge. When she disobeyed God, sinned, and ate the fruit, this knowledge only added to her sorrows. It has been that way ever since. One can have a head full of knowledge, but the heart is empty. You can know history yet not know His Story.

Life without Jesus Christ is monotonous and meaningless. Jesus is the only one who can give purpose to life. When life gets boring, see Jesus. He gives joy in life. [3]

## REMEMBER YOUR MAKER

God, you and you alone give meaning to life.

## ROAR WITH MIRTH

Attending a wedding for the first time, a little girl whispered to her mother, "Why is the bride dressed in white?" The mother replied, "Because white is the color of happiness, and today is the happiest day of her life." The child thought about this for moment, then said, "So why is the groom wearing black?"

## REFLECT ON THE MESSAGE:

Which best describes you?

- The workaholic who pursues all the world has to offer
- The alcoholic who runs from life and reality
- The one who is satisfied with Jesus

# Notes

[1] Garrett, p. 282
[2] Garrett, p.289
[3] Wiersbe, p. 34-36

# Day 4

# Wit

## READ THE MANUSCRIPT

Ecclesiastes 2:1-2, "I said in mine heart, Go to now, I will prove thee with mirth, therefore enjoy pleasure: and, behold, this also is vanity. I said of laughter, It is mad: and of mirth, What doeth it?"

## REVIEW THE MATERIAL

Solomon starts off by talking to himself. "I said in my heart." The Swiss psychologist Jean Piaget observed that toddlers begin to control their actions as soon as they start talking to themselves. When the toddlers would approach a hot surface, they would say, "hot, hot." This practice was helpful and continues to this day. Observation reveals that many sports players talk to themselves as a method to control their attitude and actions. So, there you have it: talking to yourself is Biblical. Solomon did it and it can actually be a sign of high cognitive function. [1]

As part of his quest for life or what can give meaning to life, Solomon has tried wisdom (1:17-18); now he tries wit

(2:1-2). Solomon certainly has the resources to have just about anything his heart desires. In 2:1-2, he says, "I will test mirth (laughter, wit) and enjoy pleasure."

The Hebrew culture and belief was that God made man to have a good time. Psalms 104 is a beautiful poetic psalm of how God made everything for man to enjoy. Solomon uses the word "pleasure" eight times in Ecclesiastes. *Chaphet* can be translated delights or pleasure. So, Solomon, in his pursuit for the meaning of life, tries mirth, laughter or pleasure.

God is not a killjoy. Jesus went to weddings and places people go to enjoy themselves and laugh. God gave Israel feasts and festivals to celebrate and laugh and have a good time. [2]

Solomon even wrote in Proverbs 17:22, "A merry heart doeth good like a medicine."

My family on my mother's side were big laughers. I mean, when they laughed, it could be heard for miles. I believe God wants us to laugh. In each of my devotional books I have a section of jokes. Corny as that may be, they often bring a smile, a laugh, or a groan at times.

But Solomon had to conclude that even laughter was vanity and was empty. He wanted to be, and probably was, the life of the party. He was the one people gathered around to hear his funny stories. But often the people with the loudest laugh on the outside are crying on the inside. There is a disease call The Clown Syndrome, where people are outwardly telling jokes, acting funny, and laughing, but they are hurting on the inside. Laughing is okay, but it will not satisfy or give meaning to life.

## REMEMBER YOUR MAKER

God, thank you for a beautiful world for us to enjoy. Thank you for moments of laughter.

## ROAR WITH MIRTH

A man went camping in a state park. Before leaving his car to go hiking, he left a note on the dashboard saying, "The stereo is broke." He did this to deter thieves from breaking into his older model car. When returning from his hike, the man noticed his car window was broken and the stereo was cut from the dashboard. A note was left by the thief saying, "We'll fix it."

## REFLECT ON THE MESSAGE

Go tell this joke to someone and watch them laugh.

# Notes

[1] Theconversation.com, Paloma Mari – Beffa, May 3, 2017
[2] Wiersbe, p. 39-41

# Day 5

# Wine

## READ THE MANUSCRIPT

Ecclesiastes 2:3, "I searched in my heart how to gratify my flesh with wine, while guiding my heart with wisdom, and hot to lay hold of folly, till I might see what was good for the sons of men to do under heaven all the days of their lives."

## REVIEW THE MATERIAL

Solomon sought to alleviate the pains of life by drinking alcohol. He wanted to be wise and have a good time at the same time. He wanted to have his proverbial cake and eat it, too. Solomon wanted to know if getting drunk or if drinking parties would give meaning to life and fill the emptiness of life in the face of death. [1]

Alcohol is responsible for 88,000 deaths per year in America. Many learn to drink while in college. Our culture makes drinking look fun. Commercials send a message that you are missing out if you are not drinking their brand of alcohol. [2]

The Washington Post reports that one out of eight Americans are alcoholics. They have a serious or severe problem with drinking. This results in numerous heath issues – like cirrhosis of the liver. Alcoholics usually do not fulfill their responsibilities at home, school, or work. Who wants to meet an alcoholic driving drunk on the highway?[3]

I grew up in a German community where parents put beer in a baby bottle to quiet crying babies. They used to brag on how many they could drink and not be drunk. But they did get drunk. Most people drink to get drunk, to escape the numerous pains of life.

Solomon found out drinking did not solve his problems. Nor will drinking solve the emptiness or loneliness in many people of today.

## REMEMBER YOUR MAKER

Lord, help those who are looking for help in a bottle. Help them see how getting drunk does not take away their pain.

## ROAR WITH MIRTH

A minister was planning a wedding at the close of the Sunday morning service. After the benediction he had planned to call the couple down to be married for a brief ceremony before the congregation. For the life of him, he couldn't think of the names of those who were to be married. "Will those wanting to get married please come to the front?" he requested. Immediately, nine single ladies, three widows, four widowers, and six single men stepped to the front.

## REFLECT ON THE MESSAGE

Talk to a family member or friend about the dangers of alcohol and how Jesus can help them.

# Notes

[1] Garrett, p. 291

[2] Thenewyorktimes, nytimes.com, Dec. 29, 2017, americacanwetalkaboutyourdrinking, gabrielleglaser

[3] Thewashingtonpost, oneineightamericanadultsisanalcoholic, studysaysbychristopheringraham, august11,1001

# Day 6

# Women

## READ THE MANUSCRIPT

Ecclesiastes 2:7, "I acquired male and female servants and have servants born in my house..."

Solomon acquired people as he pleased. Kings 11:1-6, "But king Solomon loved many strange women, together with the daughter of Pharaoh, women of the Moabites, Ammonites, Edomites, Zidonians, and Hittites: Of the nations concerning which the Lord said unto the children of Israel, Ye shall not go in to them, neither shall they come in unto you: for surely they will turn away your heart after their gods: Solomon clave unto these in love. And he had seven hundred wives, princesses, and three hundred concubines: and his wives turned away his heart. For it came to pass, when Solomon was old, that his wives turned away his heart after other gods: and his heart was not perfect with the Lord his God, as was the heart of David his father. For Solomon went after Ashtoreth the goddess of the Zidonians, and after Milcom the abomination of the Ammonites. And Solomon did evil in the sight of the Lord, and went not fully after the Lord, as did David his father."

Ecclesiastes 7:26-28, "And I find more bitter than death the woman, whose heart is snares and nets, and her hands as bands: whoso pleaseth God shall escape from her; but the sinner shall be taken by her. Behold, this have I found, saith the preacher, counting one by one, to find out the account: Which yet my soul seeketh, but I find not: one man among a thousand have I found; but a woman among all those have I not found."

## REVIEW THE MATERIAL

700 wives and 300 concubines is beyond our understanding. Solomon would marry to obtain more land. The trouble is that these foreign women turned his heart away from God. Mission trips to Africa afforded me the opportunity to understand some of the dynamics of Solomon's many wives. Often in Africa, there were more women than men. Men would die early in tribal wars. This left women with children without a husband and no means of support. So, a common scene was the richer a man was the more wives and children he had. I do not pretend to understand with knowledge on the degree of love in any of these marriages. It appeared that the women were viewed as property. The more wealth a man had, the more property he possessed, and that included slaves and women.

Some men in our sex-crazed culture would read 700 wives and 300 concubines and respond "WOW", and some would say "no way, I can't afford one wife, much less 1000 women!" To follow the pattern of previous verses, women were just another pursuit of Solomon to find meaning in life.

I believe every man needs a woman. I hold to that scripture that God created woman to be a helpmate to man. I believe a man is not complete until he is married. But I hold strongly to a one-woman man. Men should be faithful to one woman. Extramarital affairs and office rendezvous are sin and they are destructive. Same-sex relationships and marriages are abominable and sickening. Fantasying with pornography is destructive to any marriage. A man and a woman are to be committed to each other. To look for fulfillment outside of the bonds of marriage will be vanity, as Solomon concluded.

## REMEMBER YOUR MAKER

Lord, keep my eyes and guard my heart for only one woman, my wife.

## ROAR WITH MIRTH

We had built our dream house some years ago and furnished it with quality pieces as we could afford them. Now the delivery truck carrying the last purchase, a new bedroom suite, was pulling into the driveway. "Finally!" I exclaimed, flinging open the front door as the driver walked up to the house. "I've been waiting twelve years for this!" "Don't blame me, lady," he said. "I just got the order this morning."

## REFLECT ON THE MESSAGE

Is there any habit or thought I have that takes my devotion away from my wife or husband?

# Day 7

# Wealth

**READ THE MANUSCRIPT**

Ecclesiastes 2:8-9, "I gathered me also silver and gold, and the peculiar treasure of kings and of the provinces: I gat me men singers and women singers, and the delights of the sons of men, as musical instruments, and that of all sorts. So I was great, and increased more than all that were before me in Jerusalem: also my wisdom remained with me."

Ecclesiastes 5:10-14, "He that loveth silver shall not be satisfied with silver; nor he that loveth abundance with increase: this is also vanity. When goods increase, they are increased that eat them: and what good is there to the owners thereof, saving the beholding of them with their eyes? The sleep of a labouring man is sweet, whether he eat little or much: but the abundance of the rich will not suffer him to sleep. There is a sore evil which I have seen under the sun, namely, riches kept for the owners thereof to their hurt. But those riches perish by evil travail: and he begetteth a son, and there is nothing in his hand. "

## REVIEW THE MATERIAL

Solomon was the wealthiest man alive in his day.

2 Chronicles 1:15 describes his wealth, "and the king made silver and gold at Jerusalem as plenteous as stones, and cedar trees made he as the sycamore trees that are in the vale for abundance."

It is estimated that Solomon received $25 million annually in gold alone. 1 Kings 10 records that the Queen of Sheba brought him over $3 million as a gift (1 Kings 10:1-10).

Ed Young, pastor of Second Baptist Church in Houston said, "the most dangerous love affair any man or woman will ever experience in this life is a love affair with money."1

To be rich is not a sin. Money is an innate object. Money is a piece of paper. You cannot attribute good or evil to money. It is what you do with money that determines if it is good or evil.

If money is your pursuit in life, you will never have enough. I heard a preacher say that John D. Rockefeller, who at that time was the richest man in the world, was asked "how much is enough money?" His answer was, "another dollar." See, if you think that money will satisfy you, then you will never have enough. Solomon came to this conclusion in Ecclesiastes 5:10, "He that loveth silver shall not be satisfied with silver; nor he that loveth abundance with increase: this is also vanity."

Wealth does not last. No matter how much money you acquire in this life, not one cent will be forwarded into your next life.

Comedian Jack Benny was portrayed as a miser, a hoarder of money. He would say, "If Jack can't take it with him, Jack won't go." Well, Jack is gone from this life and his money is still here. 2

## REMEMBER YOUR MAKER

God, I acknowledge that all is yours. As the scripture states, the earth and all therein is yours. Help me to be a good steward to manage well what you have entrusted to me.

## ROAR WITH MIRTH

A wife with a depressed husband tried to cheer him up. "What do you mean you have nothing to live for? We still have to pay for the house, the car, the TV and the refrigerator!"

## REFLECT ON THE MESSAGE

What is your attitude towards money?

# Notes

[1] Young, p. 92
[2] Young, p. 99

# Day 8

# Work

**READ THE MANUSCRIPT**

Ecclesiastes 2:10-26, "And whatsoever mine eyes desired I kept not from them, I withheld not my heart from any joy; for my heart rejoiced in all my labour: and this was my portion of all my labour. Then I looked on all the works that my hands had wrought, and on the labour that I had laboured to do: and, behold, all was vanity and vexation of spirit, and there was no profit under the sun. And I turned myself to behold wisdom, and madness, and folly: for what can the man do that cometh after the king? even that which hath been already done. Then I saw that wisdom excelleth folly, as far as light excelleth darkness. The wise man's eyes are in his head; but the fool walketh in darkness: and I myself perceived also that one event happeneth to them all. Then said I in my heart, As it happeneth to the fool, so it happeneth even to me; and why was I then more wise? Then I said in my heart, that this also is vanity. For there is no remembrance of the wise more than of the fool for ever; seeing that which now is in the days to come shall all be forgotten. And how dieth the wise man? as the fool. Therefore I hated life; because the work that is wrought under the sun is grievous unto me: for all is vanity and vexation of spirit. Yea, I hated all my labour which I had taken under the sun: because I should leave it unto the man that shall be after me. And who knoweth whether he shall be a wise man or a fool? yet shall he have rule over all my labour wherein I have laboured, and wherein I have shewed myself wise under the sun. This is also vanity. Therefore I went about to cause my heart to despair of all the labour which I took under the sun. For there is a man whose labour is in wisdom, and in knowledge, and in equity; yet to a man that hath not laboured therein shall he leave it for his portion. This also is vanity and a great evil. For what hath man of all his labour, and of the vexation of his heart, wherein he hath laboured under the sun? For all his days are sorrows, and his travail grief; yea, his heart taketh not rest in the night. This is also vanity. There is nothing better for a man, than that he should eat and drink, and that he should make his soul enjoy good in his labour. This also I saw, that it was from the hand of God. For who can eat, or who else can hasten hereunto, more than I? For God giveth to a man that is good in his sight wisdom, and knowledge, and joy: but to the sinner he giveth travail, to gather and to heap up, that he may give to him that is good before God. This also is vanity and vexation of spirit. "

Ecclesiastes 4:4, "Again, I considered all travail, and every right work, that for this a man is envied of his neighbor. This is also vanity and vexation of spirit."

Ecclesiastes 5:16-20, "And this also is a sore evil, that in all points as he came, so shall he go: and what profit hath he that hath laboured for the wind? All his days also he eateth in darkness, and he hath much sorrow and wrath with his sickness. Behold that which I have seen: it is good and comely for one to eat and to drink, and to enjoy the good of all his labour that he taketh under the sun all the days of his life, which God giveth him: for it is his portion. Every man also to whom God hath given riches and wealth, and hath given him power to eat thereof, and to take his portion, and to rejoice in his labour; this is the gift of God. For he shall not much remember the days of his life; because God answereth him in the joy of his heart."

## REVIEW THE MATERIAL

Solomon is disillusioned by past pursuits to find meaning in life. He has tried:

- Wisdom – 1:17-18
- Wit – 2:1-2
- Wine – 2:3
- Women – 2:7
- Wealth – 2:8

After all these pursuits he declared, "all is vanity, useless, meaningless, empty." Now we see him in today's passage proverbially rolling up his sleeves and pursuing work to satisfy himself. Notice Ecclesiastes 2:4, "I made me great works..."

- Solomon built homes – 1 Kings 7
- Solomon built cities – 2 Chronicles 8:4-6
- Solomon built gardens - 1 Kings 4:33
- Solomon built a water system – Ecclesiastes 2:6
- Solomon built the temple - 1 Kings 5

Solomon had many workers (Ecclesiastes 2:7). Solomon had money (Ecclesiastes 2:8-9). The trouble with all that Solomon had and accomplished, he still was empty (Ecclesiastes 2:10-11).

I believe in work. I grew up in a home where my dad taught me to work. He would often say, "do something, even if it is wrong, just be working." My dad was a workaholic. Often workaholics retire and die in the first years of retirement because they feel useless.

I have very little use for lazy people. The Bible places great value on hard work. The Bible says no good thing about lazy people. I thank God that my earthly father taught me the value of work. My wife, family, and friends say I work too much. I enjoy what God has assigned to me. I thank God he allows me to rise every morning and pursue my work with passion. Yet, I know work is not to define who we are.

Have you ever noticed when you meet new people, the first two things they want to know about you?

- What is your name?
- What is your occupation?

I am Mike Smith and presently I am President of Jacksonville College. Yet being President does not define who I am. I am a Christian. I am in Christ and He is in me. This is who I am and what defines me. I do not wish to be remembered or defined by the title of my occupation. I want to be defined by who I am in Christ and His call upon my life. It is Christ working in me that will last. My work on earth is temporary.

## REMEMBER YOUR MAKER

God, help me to see you work today, not what I do as President of Jacksonville College.

## ROAR WITH MIRTH

From Reader's Digest: Shortly after I moved to a new neighborhood, my African gray parrot accidentally flew out the door. Panicked, I ran after him. One of the new words that the parrot had learned recently was coffee, and his nickname was Small. As a result, I was running around yelling "Small! Coffee!" at the trees, like a madwoman, hoping for him to squawk a response. Finally, a neighbor cautiously approached me with a steaming mug in hand and said, "Maybe you should switch to decaf, honey." Remarkably, I got my parrot back later that day.

## REFLECT ON THE MESSAGE

Who are you?

# Day 9

# Worship

## READ THE MANUSCRIPT

Ecclesiastes 2:24-26, "There is nothing better for a man, than that he should eat and drink, and that he should make his soul enjoy good in his labour. This also I saw, that it was from the hand of God. For who can eat, or who else can hasten hereunto, more than I? For God giveth to a man that is good in his sight wisdom, and knowledge, and joy: but to the sinner he giveth travail, to gather and to heap up, that he may give to him that is good before God. This also is vanity and vexation of spirit."

## REVIEW THE MANUSCRIPT

Eight times in Ecclesiastes, Solomon refers to eating and drinking and enjoying life. Up to this point, Solomon has been living a cafeteria buffet style of life. He has been picking and choosing off the table of life the things he thinks will fulfill him. He has taken a serving of wisdom, wealth, wit, women, wine, work, and now in verse 24 he says, "from the hand of

God..." He is referring to worship. Is Solomon finally getting it right? H as Solomon discovered that life is fulfilled only in the context of God?

No, sad to say, Solomon treats worship as another pursuit. Solomon's worship is by his standard, not God's design. Sad to say, many today treat worship as if going through the cafeteria buffet line. They take what they want to believe about God and leave the rest. Our culture is so against absolutes. Our culture wants only a worship experience that pleases them. Today our culture screams out "my rights." It does not matter if your god is a totem pole, a Buddha statue, Allah or Sophia. If it works for you, then our culture affirms that is your right.

What does the Bible say? It is a foreign statement in our culture. Solomon in Ecclesiastes 2:26 states, "For God giveth to a man that is good in his sight wisdom, and knowledge, and joy, but to the sinner he giveth travail, to gather and to heap up, that he may give to him that is good before God..." It appears Solomon is proclaiming Jewish theology. This is a belief held by many. God gives good to His people and evil to sinners.

The Hebrew word in this passage for God is Elohim. Elohim is the God of creation. He is an all-powerful God and man should respond to Him with reverence and respect. 1

In worship, we are not to pick and choose the kind of God we want to worship. We must worship the God of the Bible. If we limit our God as Solomon did to a God who gives good to the saints and sorrows to the sinners, we will end up as Solomon did in verse 26, "This also is vanity..."

The Bible presents a God who allows pain to come upon His people at times to correct them, to teach them, to mature them. We are not to limit our worship of God only in the good times or on the mountain tops. Worship is to take place in the sorrows of the valleys.

We are to worship God, not what he gives or does not give us.

## REMEMBER YOUR MAKER

God, help me to worship you in spirited truth, not in my flesh and the wants of life.

## ROAR WITH MIRTH

Billy Graham was returning to Charlotte after a speaking engagement and when his plane arrived, there was a limousine there to transport him to his home. As he prepared to get into the limo, he stopped and spoke to the driver. "You know", he said, "I am 87 years old and I have never driven a limousine. Would you mind if I drove it for a while?" The driver said, "No problem, have at it." Billy gets into the driver's seat and they head off down the highway. A short distance away sat a rookie State Trooper operating his first speed trap. The long black limo went by him doing 70 in a 55-mph zone. The trooper pulled out and easily caught the limo. The young trooper walked up to the driver's door and when the glass was rolled down, he was surprised to see who was driving. He immediately excused himself and sent back to his car and called his supervisor. He told the supervisor, "I know we are supposed to enforce the law...but I also know that important people are given certain courtesies. I need to know what I should do because I have stopped a very important person." The supervisor asked, "Is it the governor?" The young trooper said, "No, he's more important than that." The supervisor said, "Oh, so it's the president." The young trooper said "No, he's even more important than that." The supervisor finally aside, "Well, then, who is it?" The young trooper said, I think it's Jesus, because he's got Billy Graham for a chauffeur!"

## REFLECT ON THE MESSAGE

What is worship?

# Notes

[1] Criswell Bible, p. 760

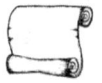

# Day 10

# Watch

**READ THE MANUSCRIPT**

Ecclesiastes 3:1-11, "To every thing there is a season, and a time to every purpose under the heaven: A time to be born, and a time to die; a time to plant, and a time to pluck up that which is planted; A time to kill, and a time to heal; a time to break down, and a time to build up; A time to weep, and a time to laugh; a time to mourn, and a time to dance A time to cast away stones, and a time to gather stones together; a time to embrace, and a time to refrain from embracing; A time to get, and a time to lose; a time to keep, and a time to cast away; A time to rend, and a time to sew; a time to keep silence, and a time to speak; A time to love, and a time to hate; a time of war, and a time of peace. What profit hath he that worketh in that wherein he laboureth? I have seen the travail, which God hath given to the sons of men to be exercised in it. He hath made every thing beautiful in his time: also he hath set the world in their heart, so that no man can find out the work that God maketh from the beginning to the end."

## REVIEW THE MATERIAL

A colleague recently sent me an email that stated, "Is it August 1?" They could not believe another semester had started. Where did all the time go?

Solomon wrote much on time. I want us to consider two important facts about time for today's devotion.

1. Time is an equalizer. We all have the same amount of time:

   - 60 seconds equals 1 minute
   - 60 minutes equals 1 hour
   - 24 hours equals 1 day
   - 365 days equals 1 year

| SECONDS: | In a Minute | In an Hour | In a Day | In a Year |
|---|---|---|---|---|
|  | 60 | 3,600 | 86,400 | 31,336,000 |

2. Time is everything.

   - Time is everything in sports. Time runs out, the buzzer is sounding, the shot is in the air. One second before it is too late. The ball works through the basketball net and the game changes. Your team has won by one point in the last second.

   - Time is everything in fishing. I recently took my grandsons on a fishing trip. We arrived at the pier to meet our guide at 5:30 a. m. He said we needed to hurry. He said a "front" would be coming in about 9 and it could get wet. We hurried up and off we went. The old adage "fish bite before a front" was true on this trip. We all started catching and soon we had our limit of big stripers. We started fishing for the smaller ones, throwing back the large ones. When our guide said it was time to go now, we might miss the rain, we left and pulled into the dock as the bottom fell out. Timing is everything in fishing.

- Timing is everything in eating on an Amtrak train ride with my grandsons. We arrived in San Antonio at midnight. They wanted to go to Mi Terra's. Mi Terra's is the largest Mexican restaurant in the world. It is open 24 hours a day. We all ordered, and we all ate too much. We had a great time. But we paid for it later. On our return trip from San Antonio to Houston, we encountered a tragedy. Near the little town of Marion, a man in a large pickup tried to outrun the train or he failed to hear or see the train and was hit by the train. One second changed or ended his life.

- April 21, 1836. Sam Houston had retreated across Texas. The Mexican army was camped on the marshlands at San Jacinto. At 3:00 p. m., while the Mexicans were having a siesta, Sam Houston attacked, and Texas was free from Mexico. Timing was everything.

- June 6, 1944. Soldiers landed on Omaha Beach on D-Day. This changed the course of the war and perhaps the world.

- John Chapter 11. Martha and Mary seem to think God was late. A close examination of the story reveals that God is never late. We need to get on His time!

## REMEMBER YOUR MAKER

God, thank you for life. Thank you for time.

## ROAR WITH MIRTH

I was sitting in my science class, when the teacher commented that the next day would be the shortest day of the year. My lab partner became visibly excited, cheering and clapping. I explained to her that the amount of daylight changes, not the actual amount of time. Needless to say, she was very disappointed.

## REFLECT ON THE MESSAGE

How can I better spend my time?

# Day 11

# Without a Mate

## READ THE MANUSCRIPT

Ecclesiastes 4:9-12, "Two are better than one; because they have a good reward for their labour. For if they fall, the one will lift up his fellow: but woe to him that is alone when he falleth; for he hath not another to help him up. Again, if two lie together, then they have heat: but how can one be warm alone? And if one prevail against him, two shall withstand him; and a threefold cord is not quickly broken.

## REVIEW THE MATERIAL

    I was ready to get married in the third grade. Jenny Sue had blond hair and sat in front of me. While other boys made ugly faces at the girls, I knew then it was a good thing to have a girlfriend. But neither of our parents would allow us to get married so I had to wait another 15 years. Warren Wiersbe points out the value of having a partner or mate in life. [1]

    1.   Life with a mate is better when it comes to working. See Verse 9. Two are better than one

because they have a good reward for their labor. When Susan and I met and fell in love we wanted to get married right away. From a pure practical point of view, it made no sense. I was making $25.00 a week pastoring a church. But Susan pointed out that she could get a job and we could make it. Many couples make it financially because both work. She did get a job at a bank near the seminary. My church gave me a raise from $25 a week to $35 a week when we got married. I told Susan $10 a week was all she could eat. She pointed out her check.

2. Life with a mate is better in walking. See Verse 10 – "For if they fall, the one will lift up his fellow: but woe to him that is alone when he falleth; for he hath not another to help him up." In life you are going to literally and figuratively fall. I literally fell in a parking lot. I messed up my shoulder. I could not use my left side. Susan helped me. She drove, carried my bags, helped me dress. I could not have made it alone. Figuratively in life, I have fallen. I have been depressed, hurt over ministry failures. Susan was always there to help life me up. I could not imagine walking through life without a mate, my mate Susan.

3. Life with a mate is better when it comes to warmth. See Verse 11 – "Again, if two lie together, then they have heat: but how can one be warm alone?" There is nothing like snuggling up to your mate on a cold night. The tradition is thought to have originated in the Netherlands. It was practiced in early colonial America by the Pennsylvania Dutch. It was a practice of fully clothed couples being wrapped in a blanket, occupying the same bed before they were married. It was called bundling. [2]

A. Life is better with a mate in watchcare. See Verse 12 – "And if one prevail against him, two shall withstand him; and a threefold cord is not quickly broken." Life is lonely and dangerous alone. Two heads are better than one. In life we need someone who has our back. Someone who looks out after us. Someone we can trust. Someone we can value their opinion. This section of Ecclesiastes is a reminder to use that we need one another, "two are better than one." I knew that in the third grade, but I am glad I waited until I found Susan.

## REMEMBER YOUR MAKER

Lord, thank you for Susan, a mate to walk through life together with

## ROAR WITH MIRTH

Fred and his wife, Edna, when to the state fair every year. Every year Fred would say, "Edna, I'd like to ride in that there airplane." And every year Edna would say, "I know, Fred, but that airplane ride costs ten dollars, and ten dollars is ten dollars."

One year, Fred and Edna went to the fair and Fred said "Edna, I'm 71 years old. If I don't ride that airplane this year, I may never get another chance." Edna replied, "Fred, that there airplane ride costs ten dollars, and ten dollars is ten dollars." The pilot overheard them and said, "Folks, I will make you a deal. I'll take you both up for a ride. If you can stay quiet for the entire ride and not say one word, I won't charge you, but if you say one word, it's ten dollars." Fred and Edna agreed and up they go.

The pilot does all kinds of twists and turns, rolls and dives, but not a word is heard. He does all his tricks over again, but still not a word. They land and the pilot turns to Fred, "By golly, I did everything I could think of to get you to yell out, but you didn't." Fred replied, "Well, I was gonna say something when Edna fell out, but ten dollars is ten dollars."

## REFLECT ON THE MESSAGE

Think back on times your mate has helped you up when you were down.

# Notes

[1] Wiersbe, p. 68-70
[2] Wikipedia

# Day 12

# World of Politics

**READ THE MANUSCRIPT**

Ecclesiastes 4:1-3, "So I returned, and considered all the oppressions that are done under the sun: and behold the tears of such as were oppressed, and they had no comforter; and on the side of their oppressors there was power; but they had no comforter. Wherefore I praised the dead which are already dead more than the living which are yet alive. Yea, better is he than both they, which hath not yet been, who hath not seen the evil work that is done under the sun."

Ecclesiastes 4:13-16, "Better is a poor and a wise child than an old and foolish king, who will no more be admonished. For out of prison he cometh to reign; whereas also he that is born in his kingdom becometh poor. I considered all the living which walk under the sun, with the second child that shall stand up in his stead. There is no end of all the people, even of all that have been before them: they also that come after shall not rejoice in him. Surely this also is vanity and vexation of spirit."

## REVIEW THE MATERIAL

Power corrupts. Solomon witnessed oppression. Solomon saw first-hand what power can do. As I write this, our nation is in the midst of preparing for an election. The President says the problem is with Congress. The Senate says the problem is with the House. The House says the problem is with the Senate. There is a lot of pointing of fingers in the world of politics.

It was said of Charles Colson that he was so loyal to President Richard Nixon that he would have run over his own grandmother to help Nixon get re-elected. [1] I have never seen the political chaos as bad we have today in America. I am concerned for our future. What can we do? We are just one.

1. 1 Timothy 2:1-6 says we are to pray for those in authority.
2. We are to obey the law. We should never think of ourselves as above the law.
3. We should seek to change law through our political process. When something is broken, we should be a part of the process to repair. We need more Christians in the political arena. I was recently invited and attended a birthday party for our U. S. Congressman. It was echoed by several speakers that we need more Christians in politics.

## REMEMBER YOUR MAKER

God, I pray for our local, state, and national leaders. Lord, give us more Christian politicians.

## ROAR WITH MIRTH

A man was on a long walk in the country. He became thirsty so he decided to stop at a little cottage and ask for something to drink. The lady of the house invited him in and served him a bowl of soup by the fire. There was a wee pig running around the kitchen, running up to the visitor and giving him a great deal of attention. The visitor commented that he had never seen a pig this friendly. The housewife replied, "Ah, he's not that friendly. That's his bowl you are using."

## REFLECT ON THE MESSAGE

What can I do today to help our political scene?

# Notes

[1] Young, p. 94

# Day 13

# Worship Without Jesus

## READ THE MANUSCRIPT

Ecclesiastes 5:1-5, "Keep thy foot when thou goest to the house of God, and be more ready to hear, than to give the sacrifice of fools: for they consider not that they do evil. Be not rash with thy mouth, and let not thine heart be hasty to utter any thing before God: for God is in heaven, and thou upon earth: therefore let thy words be few. For a dream cometh through the multitude of business; and a fool's voice is known by multitude of words. When thou vowest a vow unto God, defer not to pay it; for he hath no pleasure in fools: pay that which thou hast vowed. Better is it that thou shouldest not vow, than that thou shouldest vow and not pay."

## REVIEW THE MATERIAL

My observation is that too many approach worship too casually. We need to be careful when we worship.

Moses took off his shoes. He knew he was on holy ground. I am not advocating we literally take off our shoes. But I am advocating we have an attitude of holiness when we enter worship. Too many do church in a casual way. [1]

Solomon warns of worship without Jesus. The problem then and now is that worship is a process of our traditions and our hearts never change. This is what is meant by the sacrifice of fools. Solomon warns us in verse two about making foolish statements in our worship.

God hears a lot of prayers and many are filled with foolish statements. "Lord, help me and I will give you more than 10% in the offering."

Ed Young gives us three imperatives for true worship. [2]

1. You must be born again. John 3:7, "Marvel not that I said unto thee, Ye must be born again." Many worship in the flesh as a ritual or tradition. Worship is to be a response of our spirit back to God, who is spirit. This can only happen to those who are born again.

2. You must focus on Jesus. John 3:14, "And as Moses lifted up the serpent in the wilderness, even so must the Son of man be lifted up:" Worship is not about you. Worship is to focus on Jesus. The purpose of worship is not to make you feel good. Worship is to lift up Jesus.

3. You must worship in his manner, not yours. John 4:22-23, "Ye worship ye know not what: we know what we worship: for salvation is of the Jews. But the hour cometh, and now is, when the true worshippers shall worship the Father in spirit and in truth: for the Father seeketh such to worship him." God does not need your sacrifice. He desires your heart.

## ROAR WITH MIRTH

When a guy's printer type began to grow faint, he called a local repair shop where a friendly man informed him that the printer probably needed only to be cleaned. Because the store charged $50 for such cleanings, he told him he might be better off reading the printer's manual and trying the job himself. Pleasantly surprised by his candor, he asked, "Does your boss know that you discourage business?" "Actually, it's my boss's idea," the employee replied sheepishly. "We usually make more money on repairs if we let people try to fix things themselves first."

## REFLECT ON THE MESSAGE

How would God rate my worship?

# Notes

[1] Young, p. 118
[2] Young, pp. 122-125

# Day 14

# Wicked Politicians

## READ THE MANUSCRIPT

Ecclesiastes 5:8-9, "If thou seest the oppression of the poor, and violent perverting of judgment and justice in a province, marvel not at the matter: for he that is higher than the highest regardeth; and there be higher than they. Moreover the profit of the earth is for all: the king himself is served by the field."

## REVIEW THE MATERIAL

Solomon observed the wickedness of politicians. He witnessed corrupt politicians again here in 5:8-9 as he did in 3:16-17 and 4:1-3, oppressing the poor. Moses had condemned this in Leviticus 19:15, "Ye shall do no unrighteousness in judgment: thou shalt not respect the person of the poor, nor honor the person of the mighty: but in righteousness shalt thou judge thy neighbour" and Deuteronomy 24:17, "Thou shalt not pervert the judgment of the stranger, nor of the fatherless; nor take a widow's raiment to pledge:"

Verse 8 expresses the frustration that we often experience until this day. That is frustration with bureaucracy.

Recently our only granddaughter, Emma, was accepted into Dallas Baptist University. We gave my wife's car to her so she could have a good vehicle. We went with her to the government office to put the vehicle in her name. We were lacking a piece of paper. We went and attained the paper and got back in line, only to discover we lacked insurance in her name. We left, travelled to an insurance office to discover they were closed. We made our way to another insurance agency and for over an hour filled out the forms and secured the proper papers. On the third trip to the government agency, we were able to transfer the car into my granddaughter's name. I understand some of the bureaucracy, but I thought of several ways to make the process simpler. But they were not interested in my suggestions.

Registration at Jacksonville College goes through an annual revision. I am constantly observing the process and challenging our administration to make it simple, quick, and efficient. No one likes lines or waiting today. My supporting data is to look at the success of Amazon. Why wait in line when my book, dress, and food can be delivered to my doorstep.

Now we come to Verse 9. There are various translations to this verse. My East Texas version is, Yes, bureaucracy is tough, politicians are corrupt, bur organized government is greater than no government. Warren Wiersbe, in his commentary on this verse, quotes Lord Alton's words to Bishop Mandell Creighton in 1887. "Power tends to corrupt; absolute power corrupts absolutely. " [1]

I have traveled to forty-seven countries of the world. I have observed wicked politicians. While in one country, inflation reached such heights the people woke up one morning to the surprise that all their bank accounts were at zero. The government took what money was in the bank for the government. They added a few more zeroes to their dollar bill and kept on governing. I observed in disaster relief how millions of dollars of food, medicine, and needed supplies were shipped to a country only to have much of it lost at the port of entry. Yes, much is wrong with our country, but it is still better organized than any country I have ever observed.

The spiritual lesson is this: corruption is wrong and should be challenged. But the problem is man's heart. Without Jesus our heart is wicked. The gospel is the only thing to combat corruption.

## REMEMBER THY MAKER

Lord, I pray for every government official from the courthouse to the White House. I pray for honest politicians.

## ROAR WITH MIRTH

A Scottish mother visits her son in his New York City apartment and asks, "How do you find the Americans, son?" "Mother," says the son, "they're such noisy people. One neighbor won't stop banging his head against the wall, while the other screams and screams all night long." "Oh, son! How do you manage to put up with them?" "What can I do? I just lie in bed quietly, playing my bagpipes."

## REFLECT ON THE MESSAGE

What can I do to help corruption? Possibly get active in local politics?

# Notes

[1] Wiersbe, p. 79

# Day 15

# Wealth Cannot Satisfy

**READ THE MANUSCRIPT**

Ecclesiastes 5:10-12, "He that loveth silver shall not be satisfied with silver; nor he that loveth abundance with increase: this is also vanity. When goods increase, they are increased that eat them: and what good is there to the owners thereof, saving the beholding of them with their eyes? The sleep of a labouring man is sweet, whether he eat little or much: but the abundance of the rich will not suffer him to sleep."

**REVIEW THE MATERIAL**

The next two devotions will deal with money. Primarily, it will expose the myth than many have about money. Today's myth we will seek to expose is that money brings satisfaction. Observe, and listen to conversations. Much of the world believes that money would solve all their problems. If people did not hold to such myths, the lottery would go debunk tonight. But because many hold to this myth that money will satisfy, they will spend their last dollar on the illusion that if they hit the jackpot all their troubles are over. Wrong.

People will lie, steal, and kill for another dollar. People are obsessed with money. They dream, scream, scam, and do whatever to make another dollar. Paul warned Timothy in 1 Timothy 6:10, "For the love of money is the root of all evil: which while some coveted after, they have erred from the faith, and pierced themselves through with many sorrows."

Note something here. Money is not evil. The love of money is the root of all evil. Money in itself is an inanimate object. It is a piece of paper. You cannot attribute evil or good to money in itself. It is what I do with money that qualified it as good and evil.

People who love money will never be satisfied. Someone asked the richest man in the world, "How much is enough money?" His answer was, "Another dollar." See, if you live for money, you will never have enough money. You could win the lottery tonight and it is only a matter of time before you will want more money. Money cannot satisfy.

John D. Rockefeller was at one time the only billionaire, earning a million dollars a week. But his health failed him. He lived on crackers and milk. He could not sleep. He worried all the time. Then he started giving his money away. His health improved and he lived to the age of ninety-eight. [1]

Money will never satisfy. Jesus Christ is the only person who can fill that void in your heart.

## REMEMBER YOUR MAKER

Lord, thank you for how you provide for me. Help me to long for you, not another dollar.

## ROAR WITH MIRTH

Emily attended church with her grandmother for the first time. Before the service her grandmother gave her $1 to put in the offering plate. But when the ushers passed the offering plate, Emily didn't put the $1 in the plate. When her grandmother asked why, Emily said, "My Dad says you don't have to tip if you don't get good service."

## REFLECT ON THE MESSAGE

How can I use money to bless someone today?

# Notes

[1] Wiersbe, p. 81

# Day 16

# Wealth Cannot Give Security

**READ THE MANUSCRIPT**

Ecclesiastes 5:13-20, "There is a sore evil which I have seen under the sun, namely, riches kept for the owners thereof to their hurt. But those riches perish by evil travail: and he begetteth a son, and there is nothing in his hand. As he came forth of his mother's womb, naked shall he return to go as he came, and shall take nothing of his labour, which he may carry away in his hand. And this also is a sore evil, that in all points as he came, so shall he go: and what profit hath he that hath laboured for the wind? All his days also he eateth in darkness, and he hath much sorrow and wrath with his sickness. Behold that which I have seen: it is good and comely for one to eat and to drink, and to enjoy the good of all his labour that he taketh under the sun all the days of his life, which God giveth him: for it is his portion. Every man also to whom God hath given riches and wealth, and hath given him power to eat thereof, and to take his portion, and to rejoice in his labour; this is the gift of God. For he shall not much remember the days of his life; because God answereth him in the joy of his heart."

## REVIEW THE MATERIAL

The scene in our text is that of two wealthy men. One man is afraid of losing his money and hides all his money and becomes a miser. The second man makes unsound investments and loses his wealth. Money did not provide security for either man.

Solomon, in our text, shows the blessing of working for our wealth. Verse 19 seems to say enjoy your work and your place in life. Money cannot provide security, but God can. If we place our trust and faith in Him and let Him lead our life, then we are secure. Often when a person follows Christ and trusts Him, then He provides.

Solomon concludes with what Jesus taught in Matthew 6:33, "But seek ye first the kingdom of God, and his righteousness; and all these things shall be added unto you. "

Our security is found in our love for God. Accept Him and His will for your life. Focus more on the Giver than the gifts. Then we are secure. [1]

I have found that a good exercise for growing in faith is to give money away, random acts of kindness. I pray and when I enter a restaurant, I seek to find someone or some couple whom I can add to my bill. I tell the waitress to add their bill to mine and that I wish to remain anonymous. I often instruct the waitress that when the person asks who paid the bill to respond "God, and He wants to see you in church Sunday."

Recently Susan and I walked into a steak house restaurant. We noticed another preacher and his wife eating alone. We invited them to our table. I told them I was paying for their meal. When I got to the cashier, she informed me that someone had already paid for our meal. You cannot out give God.

## REMEMBER YOUR MAKER

God, thank you for your blessings. Help me today to be a blessing.

## ROAR WITH MIRTH

The students in a third-grade class were bombarding the teacher with questions about her newly pierced ears. "Does the hole go all the way through?" "Yes." "Did it hurt?" "Just a little." Did they stick a needed through your ears?" "No, they used a special gun." Silence followed, and then one solemn voice called out, "How far away did they stand?"

## REFLECT ON MESSAGE

How can I bless someone today?

# Notes

[1] Wiersbe, pp. 80-83

# Day 17

# Wish I Had Never Been Born

**READ THE MANUSCRIPT**

Ecclesiastes 6:1-12, "There is an evil which I have seen under the sun, and it is common among men: A man to whom God hath given riches, wealth, and honour, so that he wanteth nothing for his soul of all that he desireth, yet God giveth him not power to eat thereof, but a stranger eateth it: this is vanity, and it is an evil disease. If a man beget an hundred children, and live many years, so that the days of his years be many, and his soul be not filled with good, and also that he have no burial; I say, that an untimely birth is better than he. For he cometh in with vanity, and departeth in darkness, and his name shall be covered with darkness. Moreover he hath not seen the sun, nor known any thing: this hath more rest than the other. Yea, though he live a thousand years twice told, yet hath he seen no good: do not all go to one place? All the labour of man is for his mouth, and yet the appetite is not filled. For what hath the wise more than the fool? what hath the poor, that knoweth to walk before the living? Better is the sight of the eyes than the wandering of the desire: this is also vanity and vexation of spirit. That which hath been is named already, and it is known that it is man: neither may he contend with him that is mightier than he. Seeing there be many things that increase vanity, what is man the better? For who knoweth what is good for man in this life, all the days of his vain life which he spendeth as a shadow? for who can tell a man what shall be after him under the sun?"

## REVIEW THE MATERIAL

The scene is often too common in a house with teenage girls. An argument breaks out between a mother and her daughter. In frustration the daughter explodes, "I wish I had never been born," as she slams her door in retreat to her room. The mother stands in the hall and soaks in what she has just heard, "I wish I had never been born. " Her mind races back fourteen years. She recalls the morning sickness. She recalls the difficult days of pregnancy. She recalls the 12 hours of struggle in delivery. She recalls the days in the incubator as her baby fought for her life. She recalls the days of childhood diseases when her daughter's temperature reached unsafe highs. To hear "I wish I had never been born" caused her pain and frustration that sent this mother to her room to solace in tears and question why?

More than one Biblical character has expressed in one form or another, "I wish I had never been born."

Moses in Numbers 11:15 explodes to God, "Kill me." In the previous verse he told God, "I am not able to bear all this people alone, because it is too heavy for me."

Elijah in 1 Kings 19:4 records that "he requested for himself that he might die..." He had a great victory over the false prophets of Baal. Yet he learns that King Ahab and Jezebel had put a price on his head. He retreats to the wilderness and rests under a juniper tree and then hides in a cave wishing to die. Often after spiritual highs come spiritual lows.

In Job 3:21, in poetic prose, expresses "which long for death, but it cometh not and dig for it more than for hidden treasures." We should understand this desire in Job. He lost it all. He lost his family, his wealth, and his health.

Jeremiah 8:3 records the word of God, "Death shall be chosen rather than life by all the residue of them that remain of this evil family..." Jeremiah preached forty years for people to repent and not one repented. God allowed evil nations surrounding Jerusalem to take them captive. Death would have been better.

Paul in 2 Corinthians 1:8 says, "For we would not, brethren, have you ignorant of our trouble which came to us in Asia, that we were pressed out of measure above strength, insomuch that we despaired even of life."

When life doesn't make sense, we get frustrated and think as other before us that death would be better.

Look at Ecclesiastes 6. By Jewish standards this man had it all. Verse 2 records that God had given him riches, wealth and honor so that he wanted nothing. Verse 3 says he had many children yet Verse 4 reveals his life is empty.

This is another reminder that money, family, things, labor, food, and drink are all only temporary pleasures. They are not necessarily evil, but neither can they bring satisfaction.

How can man achieve everything he ever wanted in life and yet feel empty? God, here to Solomon and to us, is revealing our need of Him. God, then and now, disallows our ability to find satisfaction in the worlds standard to drive us to God.

How do we understand life?

1. <u>Accept God's design.</u> Verse 10 says "that which hath been is named already...neither may he contend with

him that is mightier than he." It does not pay to argue with God. He is going to win. The positive side of this verse is that God, who is the blessed controller of all things, has a plan for your life.

2. <u>Acknowledge man's departure from God's design</u>. The Bible calls this departure of man from God "sin." Sin leads to emptiness. We all have sinned and departed from God. We all sought to find meaning and fulfillment in life in all the wrong places. Only God knows the future (Verse 12), so why not yield to his plan?

## REMEMBER YOUR MAKER

God, I yield my life into your hands today. I seek you to satisfy me.

## ROAR WITH MIRTH

Mary was having a tough day and had stretched herself out on the couch to do a bit of what she thought to be well-deserved complaining and self-pitying. She moaned to her mom and brother, "Nobody loves me...the whole world hates me!" Her brother, busily occupied playing a game, hardly looked up at her and passed on this encouraging word: "That's not true, Mary. Some people don't even know you."

## REFLECT ON THE MESSAGE

What am I seeking to satisfy me?

# Day 18

# Worthy Name

**READ THE MANUSCRIPT**

Ecclesiastes 7, "A good name is better than precious ointment; and the day of death than the day of one's birth. It is better to go to the house of mourning, than to go to the house of feasting: for that is the end of all men; and the living will lay it to his heart. Sorrow is better than laughter: for by the sadness of the countenance the heart is made better. The heart of the wise is in the house of mourning; but the heart of fools is in the house of mirth. It is better to hear the rebuke of the wise, than for a man to hear the song of fools. For as the crackling of thorns under a pot, so is the laughter of the fool: this also is vanity. Surely oppression maketh a wise man mad; and a gift destroyeth the heart. Better is the end of a thing than the beginning thereof: and the patient in spirit is better than the proud in spirit. Be not hasty in thy spirit to be angry: for anger resteth in the bosom of fools. Say not thou, What is the cause that the former days were better than these? for thou dost not enquire wisely concerning this. Wisdom is good with an inheritance: and by it there is profit to them that see the sun. For wisdom is a defence, and money is a defence: but the excellency of knowledge is, that wisdom giveth life to them that have it. Consider the work of God: for who can make that straight, which he hath made crooked? In the day of prosperity be joyful, but in the day of adversity consider: God also hath set the one over against the other, to the end that man should find nothing after him. All things have I seen in the days of my vanity: there is a just man that perisheth in his righteousness, and there is a wicked man that prolongeth his life in his wickedness. Be not righteous over much; neither make thyself over wise: why shouldest thou destroy thyself? Be not over much wicked, neither be thou foolish: why shouldest thou die before thy time? It is good that thou shouldest take hold of this; yea, also from this withdraw not thine hand: for he that feareth God shall come forth of them all. Wisdom strengtheneth the wise more than ten mighty men which are in the city. For there is not a just man upon earth, that doeth good, and sinneth not. Also take no heed unto all words that are spoken; lest thou hear thy servant curse thee:

For oftentimes also thine own heart knoweth that thou thyself likewise hast cursed others. All this have I proved by wisdom: I said, I will be wise; but it was far from me. That which is far off, and exceeding deep, who can find it out? I applied mine heart to know, and to search, and to seek out wisdom, and the reason of things, and to know the wickedness of folly, even of foolishness and madness: And I find more bitter than death the woman, whose heart is snares and nets, and her hands as bands: whoso pleaseth God shall escape from her; but the sinner shall be taken by her. Behold, this have I found, saith the preacher, counting one by one, to find out the account: Which yet my soul seeketh, but I find not: one man among a thousand have I found; but a woman among all those have I not found. Lo, this only have I found, that God hath made man upright; but they have sought out many inventions."

## REVIEW THE MATERIAL

My mother gave it to me one Christmas. It hangs above my desk at home to this day. Here it is:

<u>**SMITH**</u>
*You got it from your father*
*It was all he had to give*
*So it's yours to use and cherish*
*As long as you may live*
*You may lose the watch he gave you*
*It can always be replaced*
*But a black mark on your name, son,*
*Might never be erased*
*It was clean the day you got it*
*And a worthy name to bear*
*When he got I from his father*
*There was no dishonor there*
*So be sure you use it wisely*
*After all is said and done*
*You'll be glad the name is spotless*
*When you give it to your son.*

No author is listed, but my mother's friend, Betty Mims, is the calligrapher.

Solomon in Ecclesiastes 7:1 says, "A good name is better than a precious ointment; and the day of death than the day of one's birth."

In Hebrew, the primary language of the Old Testament, the word for name is Shem. The Hebrew word for perfume is *Shemen*. Solomon is doing a play on words. He is saying a good *shem* (name) is better than *shemen* (perfume). Perfume attracts others. Solomon is saying a good name is very powerful and influential. [1]

In fact, all of Ecclesiastes 7 is a list of play on words or contrasts. He uses the word "better" eleven times. Let's do a quick glance.

1. Verse 2 – Mourning is better than feasting. Mourning confronts us with death. In death, all the shallow side issues of life are pushed aside. Reality sets in. Feasting confronts us with deceitful living. It is usually short lived and unreal.

2. Verse 3 – Sorrow is better than laughter. I do not know the origin, but I heard Ron Dunn, a preacher from Irving, Texas say:

   *I walked a mile with laughter,*

   *She chatted all the way*

   *But I was none the wiser*

   *For what laughter had to say.*

   *I walked a mile with sorrow*

   *She never said a word*

   *But O the lessons I learned from sorrow.*

3. Verse 5 – Rebuke is better than a song. A rebuke from a friend is far more helpful than a song of flattery.

4. Verse 8 – The end is better than the beginning. Don't be fooled by flashy beginnings. The long haul of life is the best.

5. Verse 10 – Today is better than yesterday. The Roman poet Horace wrote "Carpe diem", "seize the day. " Yesterday is past and cannot be changed. Tomorrow may not come, make the most of today. [2] You may wonder at times what God is doing. It seems at times good people suffer and evil people are successful.

We must remember, God is the designer. He states in Ecclesiastes 7:12 that wisdom is a defense. Living against God's design is foolish. Living with wisdom – which is seeing life from God's point of view – leads to a satisfied life. Don't look at life from your viewpoint, but look at it from God's view, then we will see what God is doing.

## ROAR WITH MIRTH

Smith goes to see his supervisor in the front office. "Boss", he says, "we're doing some heavy house-cleaning at home tomorrow, and my wife needs me to help with the attic and garage, moving and hauling stuff. " "We're short-handed, Smith," the boss replies. "I can't give you the day off. " "Thanks, boss," says Smith, "I knew I could count on you!"

## REFLECT ON THE MESSAGE

What kind of a name are you leaving your children?

# Notes

[1] Stedman, p. 87
[2] Wiersbe, p. 104

# Day 19

# Why So Much Evil

## READ THE MANUSCRIPT

Ecclesiastes 8, "Who is as the wise man? and who knoweth the interpretation of a thing? a man's wisdom maketh his face to shine, and the boldness of his face shall be changed. I counsel thee to keep the king's commandment, and that in regard of the oath of God. Be not hasty to go out of his sight: stand not in an evil thing; for he doeth whatsoever pleaseth him. Where the word of a king is, there is power: and who may say unto him, What doest thou? Whoso keepeth the commandment shall feel no evil thing: and a wise man's heart discerneth both time and judgment. Because to every purpose there is time and judgment, therefore the misery of man is great upon him. For he knoweth not that which shall be: for who can tell him when it shall be? There is no man that hath power over the spirit to retain the spirit; neither hath he power in the day of death: and there is no discharge in that war; neither shall wickedness deliver those that are given to it. All this have I seen, and applied my heart unto every work that is done under the sun: there is a time wherein one man ruleth over another to his own hurt. And so I saw the wicked buried, who had come and gone from the place of the holy, and they were forgotten in the city where they had so done: this is also vanity. Because sentence against an evil work is not executed speedily, therefore the heart of the sons of men is fully set in them to do evil. Though a sinner do evil an hundred times, and his days be prolonged, yet surely I know that it shall be well with them that fear God, which fear before him: But it shall not be well with the wicked, neither shall he prolong his days, which are as a shadow; because he feareth not before God. There is a vanity which is done upon the earth; that there be just men, unto whom it happeneth according to the work of the wicked; again, there be wicked men, to whom it happeneth according to the work of the righteous: I said that this also is vanity. Then I commended mirth, because a man hath no better thing under the sun, than to eat, and to drink, and to be merry: for that shall abide with him of his labour the days of his life, which God giveth him under the sun. When I applied mine heart to know wisdom, and to see the business that is done upon the earth: (for also there is that neither day nor night seeth sleep with his eyes:) Then I beheld all the work of God, that a man cannot find out the work that is done under the sun: because though a man labour to seek it out, yet he shall not find it; yea farther; though a wise man think to know it, yet shall he not be able to find it. "

## REVIEW THE MATERIAL

One of the ageless questions of life is why evil? If there is a God, why does He allow evil? Why do good people suffer, and evil people prosper?

Solomon does not deny the reality of evil. He often writes of it. He uses the word 22 times in Ecclesiastes. Every time it is the Hebrew word "*ra*." It carries with it many interpretations. *Ra* can mean adversity, affliction, bad calamity, distress, evil, grief, hurt, misery, pain, sorrow, trouble, wrong. [1]

Warren Wiersbe in his writing on Ecclesiastes "Be Satisfied" shares how Solomon deals with the problem of evil by examining three areas of life. I have renamed those areas but was greatly helped by his discussion.

1. Injustice
    a. Reread Ecclesiastes 8:1-9. Chapter 8 reveals the injustice in governments. The Jews often suffered at the hands of injustice. Consider their treatment under Pharaoh, Nebuchadnezzar, Edomites, Egypt, Moabites, Romans, Turks, Germany, Iraq, Iran, to this day.
    b. Solomon advised when faced with an unjust evil king, use wisdom. "Who is as the wise man? And who knoweth the interpretation of a thing?" (v. 1). "I counsel thee to keep the king's commandment..." (v. 2).
    c. In the New Testament, when Paul and the other apostles were arrested, they used spiritual discernment. The showed respect towards those in authority.
    d. When we are faced with cruel government or laws we disagree with, we have the option of disobeying, disappearing, defying orders, or demanding our rights. We need to exercise wisdom.
    e. Recent scenes at sporting event of an athlete not standing for national anthem disgusts me personally. At Jacksonville College, as long as I am President, every student will stand out of

respect or receive the call to attend another college. Do I agree with everything about our government? NO! Much is wrong in Washington. But I respect those in authority. This is what Solomon is saying in Verse 2, "I counsel thee to keep the King's commandment." Would I ever defy the king as Daniel did? Yes, but I will use wisdom to discern when that time is.

2. Inequity

   a. Reread Ecclesiastes 8:10-14. Solomon in verse 14 is saying a good man gets what a bad man should get, and a bad man gets what a good man should get. Life is not fair, but where are we ever promised that?

   b. How should a Christian respond to the inequities of this world? Similar to our response to the injustices of the world. We are to obey the law of the land. Christianity can grow in countries filled with inequity. Look at Communist China. A country filled with inequity, yet I've been told 300 people a day are responding to the gospel.

   c. Inequity is one of the vanities of life. Be cynical, pessimistic, defiant, or obey and live peaceably as much as possible.

3. Inexplainable

   a. Reread Ecclesiastes 8:15-17. A person who thinks he knows it all or has to know it all will be disappointed in this world. Solomon was a searcher for the answers of life. He concluded in 8:17 "Man cannot find out the work that is done under the sun." No man or woman will ever on this earth be able to comprehend the work of God.

b. Warren Wiersbe shares a story. "During the darkest days of World War II, somebody asked a friend of mine, "why doesn't God stop the war?" My friend wisely replied, "Because He didn't start it in the first place." [2]

## ROAR WITH MIRTH

"This house," said the real estate agent, "has both its good points and its bad points. To show you I'm honest, I'm going to tell you about both. The disadvantages are that there is a chemical plant one block south and a slaughterhouse a block north." "What are the advantages?" inquired the prospective buyer. "The advantage is that you can always tell which way the wind is blowing."

## REFLECT ON THE MESSAGE

What will be my response to evil today?

# Notes

[1] Strong's, p. 109
[2] Wiersbe, pp. 113-120

# Day 20

# Without Breath

**READ THE MANUSCRIPT**

Ecclesiastes 9:1-10," For all this I considered in my heart even to declare all this, that the righteous, and the wise, and their works, are in the hand of God: no man knoweth either love or hatred by all that is before them. All things come alike to all: there is one event to the righteous, and to the wicked; to the good and to the clean, and to the unclean; to him that sacrificeth, and to him that sacrificeth not: as is the good, so is the sinner; and he that sweareth, as he that feareth an oath. This is an evil among all things that are done under the sun, that there is one event unto all: yea, also the heart of the sons of men is full of evil, and madness is in their heart while they live, and after that they go to the dead. For to him that is joined to all the living there is hope: for a living dog is better than a dead lion. For the living know that they shall die: but the dead know not any thing, neither have they any more a reward; for the memory of them is forgotten. Also their love, and their hatred, and their envy, is now perished; neither have they any more a portion for ever in any thing that is done under the sun. Go thy way, eat thy bread with joy, and drink thy wine with a merry heart; for God now accepteth thy works. Let thy garments be always white; and let thy head lack no ointment. Live joyfully with the wife whom thou lovest all the days of the life of thy vanity, which he hath given thee under the sun, all the days of thy vanity: for that is thy portion in this life, and in thy labour which thou takest under the sun. Whatsoever thy hand findeth to do, do it with thy might; for there is no work, nor device, nor knowledge, nor wisdom, in the grave, whither thou goest."

## REVIEW THE MATERIAL

Solomon in Ecclesiastes 9:1-10 is saying that it does not matter:
- How wise you are
- How rich you are
- How secure you are
- How successful you are
- How comfortable you are

Death is coming.

Solomon in these verses gives us an analysis of death. [1] Woody Allen, the entertainer, said "I'm not afraid to die," "I just don't want to be there when it happens." But he will be.

Life and death are in God's hands (V. 1). Death is not an accident; it is an appointment. Hebrews 9:27 says, "And as it is appointed unto men once to die, but after this the judgment:"

Death is coming whether you are good or bad (V. 2). How people face death is really like a reflection of how they faced life.

How do people face death?

1. Deny it (Verse 3)

Some people deny death. They do not want to talk about it. If you bring up the subject, they quickly change the subject. Some people really think they are going to live forever. It amazes me as I have dealt with numerous Christian families through the years who did not prepare for death. Death came and they had no will, no cemetery plot, no burial insurance or instructions. I am not bragging, but Susan and I have our death plans in place. We have a will. Our cemetery plot. We have our tombstone marker with everything on it but the day of death. We have the service already paid for. We have detailed instructions given to the undertaker. I've even given him the slides to show before the service. I have the scripture and songs chosen. I have my pallbearers listed. They are to be: 2 of the meanest deacons I ever had to pastor; 2 of the laziest pastors I ever had to work with in the association; and 2 of the stingiest trustees I've ever had on the college board.

I have the length of service to the minute and I have money set aside to pay for a BBQ rib dinner for everyone. I don't want to leave any of the worry of planning to my family.

I joke and freely talk about death. Yes, there is sorrow and crying at the death of a loved one, but it does not have to be ungodly sorrow as some do without hope. Because of my faith and hope in Jesus, I have not denied the reality of death.

2. Deal with Death (Verses 4-10)

Solomon says in these verses to deal with death. Get up and enjoy life. In verse seven, he says enjoy your meals. In verse eight, enjoy life and in verse nine, enjoy your marriage, and in verse ten, enjoy your work.

When you are a Christian, your life after death is settled. You have a hope, a future. So, the emphasis in this life does not have to be worrying about the future. The emphasis now is on knowing and doing the will of God.

Once the question of where you spend eternity is secured, then your focus is on living the Christ-like life in the here and now.

## REMEMBER YOUR MAKER

God, because you live, I have a hope secured in Christ.

## ROAR WITH MIRTH

An atheist was walking through the woods. As he was walking alongside the river, he heard a rustling in the bushes behind him. He turned to look. He saw a 7-foot grizzly bear charging towards him. He ran as fast as he could up the path. He looked over his shoulder and saw the bear was closing in on him. He looked over his shoulder again and the bear was even closer. He tripped and fell on the ground. He rolled over to pick himself up, but saw the bear was right on top of him; reaching for him with his left paw and raising his right paw to strike him. At that instant, the atheist cried out, "Oh my God!" Time stopped. The bear froze. The forest was silent. As a bright light shone upon the man a voice came out of the sky, "you deny my existence for all these years, teach others I don't exist and even credit creation to a cosmic accident. Do you really expect me to help you out of this predicament?" The atheist looked directly into the light and said, "It would be hypocritical of me to suddenly ask you to treat me as a Christian now, but perhaps you could make the BEAR a

Christian?" "Very well," said the voice. The light went out. The sounds of the forest resumed. And the bear dropped his right paw, brought both paws together, bowed his head and spoke: "Lord, bless this food which I am about to receive from Thy bounty through Christ our Lord, Amen."

## REFLECT ON THE MESSAGE

Are my plans of death arranged, such as the funeral, the service, etc.?

# Notes

[1] Akin, p. 100

# Day 21

# World of Surprises

## READ THE MANUSCRIPT

Ecclesiastes 9:11-18, "I returned, and saw under the sun, that the race is not to the swift, nor the battle to the strong, neither yet bread to the wise, nor yet riches to men of understanding, nor yet favour to men of skill; but time and chance happeneth to them all. For man also knoweth not his time: as the fishes that are taken in an evil net, and as the birds that are caught in the snare; so are the sons of men snared in an evil time, when it falleth suddenly upon them. This wisdom have I seen also under the sun, and it seemed great unto me: There was a little city, and few men within it; and there came a great king against it, and besieged it, and built great bulwarks against it: Now there was found in it a poor wise man, and he by his wisdom delivered the city; yet no man remembered that same poor man. Then said I, Wisdom is better than strength: nevertheless the poor man's wisdom is despised, and his words are not heard. The words of wise men are heard in quiet more than the cry of him that ruleth among fools. Wisdom is better than weapons of war: but one sinner destroyeth much good."

## REVIEW THE MATERIAL

Forest Gump in the movie by the same name would often say, "Life is like a box of chocolates, you never know what you are going to get."

Solomon is saying the same thing in Ecclesiastes 9:11-18.

Normally, the fastest runner wins the race. Normally, the strongest soldiers win the battles. Normally, the smartest workers get the job promotions. But that's not always the case. Warren Wiersbe says the word chance in Verse 11 means occurrence or event. It has nothing to do with gambling. He quotes, "I just happened to be in the right place at the right time, and I got the job. Ability had very little to do with it."[1]

As a Christian, I place my life in the providence of God. I pray and trust God in my decision-making process. I do not leave my life up to luck or chance.

We are not clear about the illustration Solomon uses in Verses 13-18. It seems to say that a city was under attack and a quiet wise man could have delivered the city, but a loudmouth ruler led them into defeat. The opportunity for success was there but one loudmouth destroyed that opportunity.

In the context of this chapter on death, Solomon is saying life and death will surprise you. As I write this, one of our students at Jacksonville College received word that her father had a heart attack and died unexpectedly. He woke up that morning and went to work but died. This caught family and friends by surprise.

We as Christians do not have to fear death and when it comes, we are not defeated. Paul said in 1 Corinthians 15:57-58, "But thanks be to God, which giveth us the victory through our Lord Jesus Christ. Therefore, my beloved brethren, be ye stedfast, unmoveable, always abounding in the work of the Lord, forasmuch as ye know that your labour is not in vain in the Lord."

## REMEMBER OUR MAKER

Lord, thank you for conquering death. Thank you for the truth that because you live, we also shall live.

## ROAR WITH MIRTH

Although this married couple enjoyed their new fishing boat together, it was the husband who was behind the wheel, operating the boat. Still, he was concerned about what might happen in an emergency. So, one day out on the lake he said to his wife, "Honey, take the wheel...pretend that I am having a heart attack. You must get the boat safely to shore and dock it." So, she drove the boat to shore and safely docked it. Later that evening, the wife walked into the living room where her husband was reading a novel. She sat down next to him, switched the TV channel, and said to him, "Honey, go into the kitchen. Pretend I'm having a heart attack and set the table, cook dinner and wash the dishes."

## REFLECT ON THE MESSAGE

Am I ready for death? Whom do I know that is not ready for death that I need to share the gospel with?

# Notes

[1] Wiersbe, pp. 130-131

# Day 22

# World Leaders

## READ THE MANUSCRIPT

Ecclesiastes 10:1-7, "Dead flies cause the ointment of the apothecary to send forth a stinking savour: so doth a little folly him that is in reputation for wisdom and honour. A wise man's heart is at his right hand; but a fool's heart at his left. Yea also, when he that is a fool walketh by the way, his wisdom faileth him, and he saith to every one that he is a fool. If the spirit of the ruler rise up against thee, leave not thy place; for yielding pacifieth great offences. There is an evil which I have seen under the sun, as an error which proceedeth from the ruler: Folly is set in great dignity, and the rich sit in low place. I have seen servants upon horses, and princes walking as servants upon the earth."

## REVIEW THE MATERIAL

Peter Drucker, the late leadership guru, said that the four hardest jobs in America are:
- President of the United States

- A university President
- A CEO of a hospital
- A Pastor[1]

Being a leader is tough. You really cannot win. No matter what direction you lead, there will be those who point out how you should have taken the other road. When things go right, you have friends. When things go wrong, you have less friends.

Solomon in our devotional passage for today is stressing how leaders need wisdom.

Fellow Texan and President of the United States, Lyndon B. Johnson, said, "A President's hardest task is not to do what's right, but to know what's right." That required wisdom. 2

Solomon points out two dangers in leadership:

1. Irate

> Verse 4, "If the spirit of the leader rises up against thee..." Anger will cause a person to lost control of a situation. Solomon in Proverbs reminded us of this several times:
>
> - Proverbs 25:28, "He that hath no rule over his own spirit is like a city that is broken down, and without walls."
> - Proverbs 16:32, "He that is slow to anger is better than the mighty; and he that ruleth his spirit than he that taketh a city."
> - Proverbs 16:14, "The wrath of a king is as messengers of death: but a wise man will pacify it."

Every leader gets frustrated and angry, but he must be under control. If a leader cannot control himself, he cannot lead effectively.

2. Indecisive

> 1 Kings 12:1-24 tells how Solomon's son, Rehoboam, was indecisive and the nation divided. Solomon, contrasting wise and foolish, points out how foolish leaders will make bad decisions. Young men on horses and the elderly walking is not the right picture. If a leader makes bad decisions, he will put the wrong people in places of leadership. The best leaders will be toughminded and tenderhearted.
>
> As Christian leaders, in our decision-making process, we have prayer, scripture, and the Holy Spirit to guide us.
>
> A Christian leader shared in a conference I attended as a youth the definition of wisdom. He said wisdom is seeing life from God's point of view. Every Christian, leader or not, should seek God's point of view in every decision.

## REMEMBER YOUR MAKER

Lord, help me to make wise decisions today.

## ROAR WITH MIRTH

A North Carolina State Trooper pulled a car over on US 301 about 2 miles south of the Virginia line. When the trooper asked the driver why he was speeding, the driver said he was a juggler and was on his way to do a show in Emporia and he didn't want to be late. The trooper told the driver that he was fascinated by juggling and if the driver would do a little juggling for him, he would not give him a ticket. The driver said he had sent all his equipment ahead and didn't have anything to juggle. The trooper said he had some flares in the trunk of the patrol car he could use. The trooper got out 5 flares, lit them, and handed them to the driver. While the man was juggling, a car pulled in behind the police car. A drunken good old boy got out, watched the performance, and then went over to the police car and got in the back seat. The trooper observed him and went over to the patrol car, opened the door and asked the guy what he thought he was doing. The drunk replied, "You might as well take me to jail, 'cause there ain't no way I could ever pass that test!"

## REFLECT ON THE MESSAGE

What decisions do I need to make? What would God do?

# Notes

[1] Churchleaders.com Thesecretpainofpastorsbyphilipwagner

[2] Wiersbe, p. 136

# Day 23

# Warnings to Workers

## READ THE MANUSCRIPT

Ecclesiastes 10:8-11, "He that diggeth a pit shall fall into it; and whoso breaketh an hedge, a serpent shall bite him. Whoso removeth stones shall be hurt therewith; and he that cleaveth wood shall be endangered thereby. If the iron be blunt, and he do not whet the edge, then must he put to more strength: but wisdom is profitable to direct. Surely the serpent will bite without enchantment; and a babbler is no better."

## REVIEW THE MATERIAL

Solomon in our text for the day is giving a warning to workers. Every worker must understand his situation, his surroundings, and his skill, or he will get into trouble.

First, we are given a picture of a man digging a well (Verse 8). The trouble is he fell into the pit. Why? He failed to notice his surroundings. I was driving a commercial truck one day. I took my eye off the road and ended up in a rice canal ditch outside Katy, Texas. I simply did not pay attention to the fact that I was driving in an area with deep ditches on each side of the road. I was foolish to take my eye off the road. The result was that my truck and I were buried in water and mud. We both survived, but it was a painful lesson.

In life, you must be aware of your surroundings. Be aware of the company you keep. Many a college student started keeping company with the wrong crowd and, before he realized it, he was deeper into sin than he ever wanted to be. Several preachers have used the following phrase:

- Sin will keep you longer than you wanted to stay.

- Sin will take you deeper than you wanted to go.

- Sin will cost you more than you wanted to pay.

Pay attention to your surroundings.

The second picture is a man who cut through a hedge and a snake bit him (Verse 8). In Verse 9 we see a man who is careless in cutting stone and wood. Snakes are often in piles of brush. The man did not pay attention to his situation. Several times in life, in the process of cleaning, I have removed a pile of limbs or boards to discover a snake's den. If I had not paid attention, I could have been hurt. Several times I walked up and the thought came to my mind: snake, that looks like a snake's home. When one is working, he cannot afford to be careless. Carelessness will cost you. Many situations in life afford dangers. As we grow in wisdom and experience, we become aware of the dangers and can avoid hurts in life.

The next picture in Verse 10 is of a foolish worker trying to split wood with a dull axe. A wise worker knows when to stop and sharpen his axe. My dad used to say, "Don't work harder, work smarter." My heritage on both sides of my parents were woodsmen. Both of my grandfathers cut timber and hauled logs for a living. They knew the value of a sharp axe and sharp chainsaw. It is a skill to know how to sharpen an axe. In life we had better acquire a set of skills if we are going to progress in our occupation. In education, you had better obtain a masters or doctorate degree. In sales, you better learn how to close the deal. In baseball, you better learn to hit the curve ball. The more skill sets you possess, the more valuable and marketable you will be.

The last picture is that of a snake charmer in Verse 11. Solomon describes a person who was bitten by a snake before he had time to charm the snake. Timing is everything. To rush into a situation can cost you. Learning to wait for the right time oven proves to be the right path. Often in life, I wanted something, but the time was not right. By waiting, it proved to be more advantageous. When I rushed into a situation, it often cost me.

In summary, Solomon says to be a wise worker. Know your situation, know your surroundings, know your skills, and know when the time is right.

## REMEMBER YOUR MAKER

God, help me to be a wise worker today.

## ROAR WITH MIRTH

A young lady was weed whacking her yard and accidentally cut off the tail of her cat, who was hiding in the grass. She rushed her cat, along with the tail, to Wal-Mart. When asked why she had brought the cat to Wal-Mart, she replied, "Helloooooo! Wal-Mart is the largest re-tailer in the world!"

## REFLECT ON THE MESSAGE

What skills do I need to acquire to be a better servant for our Lord?

# Day 24

# Wagging Tongues

## READ THE MANUSCRIPT

Ecclesiastes 10:12-15, "The words of a wise man's mouth are gracious; but the lips of a fool will swallow up himself. The beginning of the words of his mouth is foolishness: and the end of his talk is mischievous madness. A fool also is full of words: a man cannot tell what shall be; and what shall be after him, who can tell him? The labour of the foolish wearieth every one of them, because he knoweth not how to go to the city."

## REVIEW THE MATERIAL

Solomon wrote a lot about speech. Proverbs is full of little pithy, pointed statements about speech.

- Proverbs 10:19, "In the multitude of words there wanteth not sin: but he that refraineth his lips is wise."

- Proverbs 15:4, "A wholesome tongue is a tree of life: but perverseness therein is a breach in the spirit."

- Proverbs 15:28, "The heart of the righteous studieth to answer: but the mouth of the wicked poureth out evil things."

- Proverbs 17:9, "He that covereth a transgression seeketh love; but he that repeateth a matter separateth very friends."

- Proverbs 21:23, "Whoso keepeth his mouth and his tongue keepeth his soul from troubles."

Likewise, in Ecclesiastes he gives us warning of wagging tongues. Verse 12 speaks of destructive speech. We may try to hurt others by slander or angry words, but we really only destroy ourselves. Verse 13 warns about a man who, the longer he talks the madder he gets. Have you ever known anyone that picture describes? It seems the more he hears himself, the more courage he obtains. Before long he has said things he did not intend to say, and he says things he cannot take back.

There is humor in these verses. Verses 14-15 describes a man who brags about his future plans, but he cannot find his way to town. It is a picture of a man who is talking so much about what he is going to do in the future, he loses his way in the present. I've known several in my life who spoke of dreams, visions, and goals for the future but were doing nothing in the present. I've known preachers who spoke of one day pastoring that mega church in the future. Yet, they were not even teaching Sunday School today.

I've known of those who spoke of going to the other side of the world to be missionaries, who today would not even go across the street to share Christ. This is the picture Solomon has painted here. Be careful in our speech.

## REMEMBER OUR MAKER

Lord, please guard my speech today.

## ROAR WITH MIRTH

A fourth-grade teacher was giving her pupils a lesson in logic. "Here is the situation," she said. "A man is standing up in a boat in the middle of a river, fishing. He loses his balance, falls in, and begins splashing and yelling for help. His wife hears the commotion, knows he can't swim, and runs down to the bank. "Why do you think she ran to the bank?" A girl raised her hand and asked, "To draw out all his savings?"

## REFLECT ON THE MESSAGE

Am I just talking about the future or am I doing today what God would have me do?

# Day 25

# Washington

## READ THE MANUSCRIPT

Ecclesiastes 10:16-20, "Woe to thee, O land, when thy king is a child, and thy princes eat in the morning! Blessed art thou, O land, when thy king is the son of nobles, and thy princes eat in due season, for strength, and not for drunkenness! By much slothfulness the building decayeth; and through idleness of the hands the house droppeth through. A feast is made for laughter, and wine maketh merry: but money answereth all things. Curse not the king, no not in thy thought; and curse not the rich in thy bedchamber: for a bird of the air shall carry the voice, and that which hath wings shall tell the matter."

## REVIEW THE MATERIAL

In this section, Solomon is describing governments. That is why I titled it Washington. Some governments are led by people who are incompetent, impulsive, insecure, and ignorant. [1]

Woodrow Wilson wrote, "A friend of mine says that every man who takes office in Washington either grows or swells; when I give a man an office, I watch him carefully to see whether he is swelling or growing."²

History records countless good men who were elected to a position and Washington corrupted them. Let's review the dangers of how leadership can corrupt a man.

1. Self-Indulgence. Verse 16

   In the Hebrew culture, the princes were to judge the problems of the people. Then at night they could feast. Here Solomon describes the judges feasting in the morning. They were self-indulging. They were not serving the people as they were appointed to do. They were self-serving. Verse 17 tells us a nation is blessed when its leaders do their job but cursed when they self-indulge in drunkenness.

2. Self-Idleness. Verse 18

   This verse describes a lazy leader. Solomon compares a nation to a house. The house is falling apart, the roof is leaking (droppeth through) because the owner is lazy, idle, and does nothing. Solomon applies this to a nation. When national leaders are lazy and do not fix the problems of our nation, then government begins to crumble. The nation becomes weak and an easy target for invasion. My grandmother used to say, "An idle mind is the devil's workshop." I have never had patience with lazy people. I certainly have no respect for lazy leaders.

3. Self-Indifference. Verse 19

   This describes a leader who wants the position to promote his desires. He is indifferent to the needs of the people who elected him. History records leaders who stole government funds in order to build their own kingdom. Verse 19 is a scene that describes a person who eats and drinks and gets more money to satisfy himself. He is totally indifferent to the needs of others.

4. Self-Indiscretion. Verse 20

Have you ever heard the saying "A little bird told me?" Read Ecclesiastes 10:20 again. This proverbial saying very well may have come from this verse. [3] Ray Stedman says this may have been the first instance of government bugging a house. It clearly reflects that "even the walls have ears."[4]

In conclusion, I do not want to be guilty of the warning in Verse 20 about cursing the king. I am very concerned about what is taking place in Washington. I have never seen our nation so divided. We truly have some godly elected officials who are trying. But there is such hatred for each other, the good of the nation goes neglected.

So, what am I to do?

- Pray for those in leadership. Romans 13, "Let every soul be subject unto the higher powers. For there is no power but of God: the powers that be are ordained of God. Whosoever therefore resisteth the power, resisteth the ordinance of God: and they that resist shall receive to themselves damnation. For rulers are not a terror to good works, but to the evil. Wilt thou then not be afraid of the power? do that which is good, and thou shalt have praise of the same: For he is the minister of God to thee for good. But if thou do that which is evil, be afraid; for he beareth not the sword in vain: for he is the minister of God, a revenger to execute wrath upon him that doeth evil. Wherefore ye must needs be subject, not only for wrath, but also for conscience sake. For this cause pay ye tribute also: for they are God's ministers, attending continually upon this very thing. Render therefore to all their dues: tribute to whom tribute is due; custom to whom custom;

fear to whom fear; honour to whom honour. Owe no man any thing, but to love one another: for he that loveth another hath fulfilled the law. For this, Thou shalt not commit adultery, Thou shalt not kill, Thou shalt not steal, Thou shalt not bear false witness, Thou shalt not covet; and if there be any other commandment, it is briefly comprehended in this saying, namely, Thou shalt love thy neighbour as thyself. Love worketh no ill to his neighbour: therefore love is the fulfilling of the law. And that, knowing the time, that now it is high time to awake out of sleep: for now is our salvation nearer than when we believed. The night is far spent, the day is at hand: let us therefore cast off the works of darkness, and let us put on the armour of light. Let us walk honestly, as in the day; not in rioting and drunkenness, not in chambering and wantonness, not in strife and envying. But put ye on the Lord Jesus Christ, and make not provision for the flesh, to fulfil the lusts thereof."

- Respect the office even when I cannot respect the person. 1 Peter 2:13-17, "Submit yourselves to every ordinance of man for the Lord's sake: whether it be to the king, as supreme; Or unto governors, as unto them that are sent by him for the punishment of evildoers, and for the praise of them that do well. For so is the will of God, that with well doing ye may put to silence the ignorance of foolish men: As free, and not using your liberty for a cloke of maliciousness, but as the servants of God. Honour all men. Love the brotherhood. Fear God. Honour the king."

- Vote.

## REMEMBER YOUR MAKER

God, I pray for all elected officials in our city, state, and nation.

## ROAR WITH MIRTH

A boss tells a job applicant, "I'll give you $8 an hour, starting today, and in three months, I'll raise it to $10 an hour. So, when would you like to start?" The applicant replied, "After three months, sir."

## REFLECT ON THE MESSAGE

How involved am I in praying for our leaders?

# Notes

[1] Stedman, p. 158
[2] Wiersbe, p. 141
[3] Stedman, p. 161
[4] Stedman, p. 161

# Day 26

# What Is Life About?

## READ THE MANUSCRIPT

Ecclesiastes 11:1-6, "Cast thy bread upon the waters: for thou shalt find it after many days. Give a portion to seven, and also to eight; for thou knowest not what evil shall be upon the earth. If the clouds be full of rain, they empty themselves upon the earth: and if the tree fall toward the south, or toward the north, in the place where the tree falleth, there it shall be. He that observeth the wind shall not sow; and he that regardeth the clouds shall not reap. As thou knowest not what is the way of the spirit, nor how the bones do grow in the womb of her that is with child: even so thou knowest not the works of God who maketh all. In the morning sow thy seed, and in the evening withhold not thine hand: for thou knowest not whether shall prosper, either this or that, or whether they both shall be alike good."

## REVIEW THE MATERIAL

Solomon began Ecclesiastes with the question, "What is life about?" "Is life worth living?" Ecclesiastes 1:3, "What profit hath a man of all his labour?" He sets out on a search or experiment with life. He tries wealth, wisdom, wit, wine, women and numerous other worldly attractions to find meaning to life. He concludes it is all vanity or empty.

Now Solomon reviews his research and this time brings God into the equation. He presents four pictures of life with God. In our passage today, Ecclesiastes 11:1-6, he concludes life is a surprise so live it by faith.

I have observed many old people. As they grow old, they seem to be more critical and contrary. I pray to God that I don't want to be like that. God give me grace to grow old. I want life to be an adventure up to the end. I do not want to sit around in a mundane existence, bored to death. Ever since I trusted Jesus as my Savior, life has been a surprise. Solomon uses two activities to illustrate his point that life is a surprise and we are to live it by faith.

1. Sailors Verses 1-2

    "Cast your bread upon the waters" was a way of saying send your harvest out to sea to be traded. You won't know what price you get until the ship returns. Any farming is a step of faith. You can plant, cultivate, and harvest, but you never know what the market is going to pay.

    Verse two could be sound advice. Put your harvest in seven or eight ships. Do not put all your eggs in one basket.

2. The Soil Tenders Verses 3-6

    Daniel Webster called farmers "the founders of civilization." Thomas Jefferson said they were "the chosen people of God." [1] Farming is tough. You have to live it by faith. It seems you are always waiting on the rain. I lived in West Texas for seven years. The dry-land cotton farmers used to say they could survive with one good crop every five years. They never knew when that good crop was coming. Just as Verse 5 says no one knows the way of the wind.

God has a time and purpose for everything. We saw that in chapter 3. So, we must accept life is a surprise and live if by faith. Enjoy life. Don't gripe but praise God for another day.

## REMEMBER YOUR MAKER

God, thank you for life. Help me to live it to the fullest.

## ROAR WITH MIRTH

A young woman was on vacation in the depths of Louisiana. She wanted a pair of genuine alligator shoes but didn't want to pay the high prices. After unsuccessfully haggling with one of the shopkeepers, the young woman said, "Maybe I'll just go out and catch my own alligator, so I can get a pair of shoes at a reasonable price." Later in the day, the shopkeeper spotted the young woman standing in waist deep water, shotgun in hand. She took aim at an alligator, killed it, and hauled it onto the swamp bank. Lying nearby were several more of the dead creatures. The shopkeeper watched in amazement as the young women flipped the alligator on its back and shouted in frustration, "This one isn't wearing any shoes, either!"

## REFLECT ON THE MESSAGE

What can I say today to be positive and thankful and not be critical or negative?

*Dr. Mike Smith*

# Notes

[1] Wiersbe, pp. 149-150

# Day 27

# What a Song

## READ THE MANUSCRIPT

Ecclesiastes 11:7-10, "Truly the light is sweet, and a pleasant thing it is for the eyes to behold the sun: But if a man live many years, and rejoice in them all; yet let him remember the days of darkness; for they shall be many. All that cometh is vanity. Rejoice, O young man, in thy youth; and let thy heart cheer thee in the days of thy youth, and walk in the ways of thine heart, and in the sight of thine eyes: but know thou, that for all these things God will bring thee into judgment. Therefore remove sorrow from thy heart, and put away evil from thy flesh: for childhood and youth are vanity."

## REVIEW THE MATERIAL

Every day we should wake up and sing a song of rejoicing unto God. I will never forget the first time I heard a man pray, "God, thank you for waking me up this morning." He was thankful to God for another day. In our text, Solomon tells us to rejoice. In Verse 8, we are to rejoice in all of life. In Verse 9, he reminds the youth to rejoice.

What a joy to be alive and given another day. Some people wake up and say, "O Lord, another day." They dread the things of life. Some wake up and say, "Good Lord, think you for a new day." These people are ready for the day.

Solomon especially taught young people to enjoy their youth. He knew that soon darkness, old age, would come. Face the fact that there are things you can do as a youth that you cannot do as an old man.

Recently I took my grandsons on a Paw Paw trip. One of our activities was an amusement park in Galveston. My grandson rode all the rides. I was amazed. These rides turned them upside down, slung them around and around and they kept getting on them for another ride. In my youth, I would have been on every ride. Today I watch from a park bench. My 70-year old body just could not take the abuse. Enjoy your youth.

It concerns me when some parents try to make their children grow up too soon. They do not let them be children. At Jacksonville College, I've seen the emotional scars of those who had no youth and were forced to be an adult before their time.

Today, I see old people trying to act like young people. It is a hideous sight. No matter how they try, their old bodies won't let them wiggle like they could at sixteen.

Enjoy each stage and age of life. Warren Wiersbe tells of a ninety-year old friend, who, on one of their visits, said, "I don't go out much not because my parents won't let me – Mother Nature and Father Time!" [1] I don't want to sit in a rocking chair until it's time to die. As long as God will give me strength, I want to get up and rejoice and serve Him.

## REMEMBER YOUR MAKER

God, thank you for another day. Give me strength to praise you!

## ROAR WITH MIRTH

A Sunday School teacher was teaching the Ten Commandments to the children in her class. After explaining the commandment to "Honor you father and mother," she asked, "Is there a commandment that teaches us how to treat our brothers and sisters?" Without missing a beat, one little boy answered, "Thou shall not kill."

## REFLECT ON THE MESSAGE

This is the day the Lord has made, and I will rejoice in it!

# Notes

[1] Wiersbe, p. 151

# Day 28

# What a Senior Citizen

### READ THE MANUSCRIPT

Ecclesiastes 12:1-8, "Remember now thy Creator in the days of thy youth, while the evil days come not, nor the years draw nigh, when thou shalt say, I have no pleasure in them; While the sun, or the light, or the moon, or the stars, be not darkened, nor the clouds return after the rain: In the day when the keepers of the house shall tremble, and the strong men shall bow themselves, and the grinders cease because they are few, and those that look out of the windows be darkened, And the doors shall be shut in the streets, when the sound of the grinding is low, and he shall rise up at the voice of the bird, and all the daughters of musick shall be brought low; Also when they shall be afraid of that which is high, and fears shall be in the way, and the almond tree shall flourish, and the grasshopper shall be a burden, and desire shall fail: because man goeth to his long home, and the mourners go about the streets: Or ever the silver cord be loosed, or the golden bowl be broken, or the pitcher be broken at the fountain, or the wheel broken at the cistern. Then shall the dust return to the earth as it was: and the spirit shall return unto God who gave it. Vanity of vanities, saith the preacher; all is vanity."

## REVIEW THE MATERIAL

I am a senior citizen. I am on Medicare. I am a member of AARP. I still get up and go to work and draw a check from my employer, but I am near 70. Officially, they say you are a senior citizen at age 55. Many retire and draw Social Security at age 65. I am not fighting old age. I just want to serve the Lord until he calls me home. I want to be busy for Him. So, at 70 I am a college President. I have dreams of a 5$^{th}$ wheel camper and a dually pickup. No, not to see the National Parks. But to go to the little dying churches and preach that these bones can live again. Ecclesiastes gives us a picture of a senior citizen:

- Verse 3 – Keepers of the house may tremble. That refers to your arms and legs.

- Verse 3 – Strong men shall bow. That is a picture of many old men who walk bent over.

- Verse 3 – Grinders cease because they are few. As you get older, you start to lose your teeth.

- Verse 3 – Those who look out of the windows be darkened. Your vision grows dim in old age.

- Verse 4 – Doors shall be shut in the streets. Your hearing starts to fail you.

- Verse 4 – The sound of the grinding is low. You have a hard time chewing.

- Verse 4 – Rise up at the voice of a bird. You can't sleep. You wake up early. I am writing this at 3 a. m. because I don't sleep much anymore. It is biblical.

- Verse 4 – Your musick shall be brought low. Your voice starts to quaver.

- Verse 5 – You are afraid of heights. Every time you go to the doctor, he asks, "Have you fallen lately?" It's not the falling that I fear, I fear no one can help me up.

- Verse 5 – The almond tree shall flourish. If you have hair, it turns white.

- Verse 5 – The grasshopper shall be a burden. You can't hop anymore. You just drag yourself along like grasshoppers do at the end of summer.

- Verse 5 – Desire shall fail. You lose your sexual desire, or it fails you.

- Verse 5 – You goeth to your long home. You go to heaven and people mourn.

- Verse 6 – Your silver cord is loosed and your golden bowl is broken. The money begins to play out in old age.

- Verse 6 – The pitcher be broken at the fountain or the wheel broken at the cistern. Our body parts cease to function. The kidneys get weak. The heart slows its circulation.

- Verse 7 – The dust returns to the earth; the spirit returns to God. Death comes to one and all.

- Verse 8 – Vanity of vanities, saith the preacher, all is vanity. Life under the sun without God is vanity. [1]

# REMEMBER YOUR MAKER

God, help me grow old graciously.

## ROAR WITH MIRTH

While on a road trip, an elderly couple stopped at a roadside restaurant for lunch. After finishing their meal, they left the restaurant, and resumed their trip. When leaving, the elderly woman unknowingly left her glasses on the table, and she didn't miss them until they had been driving for about 40 minutes. By then, to add to the aggravation, they had to travel quite a distance before they could find a place to turn around, in order to return to the restaurant to retrieve her glasses. All the way back, the elderly husband became the classic grumpy old man. He fussed and complained and scolded his wife relentlessly during the entire return drive. The more he chided her, the more agitated he became. He just wouldn't let up for a single minute. To her relief, they finally arrived at the restaurant. As the woman got out of the car, and hurried inside to retrieve her glasses, the old geezer yelled out to her, "While you're in there, you might as well get my hat and the credit card!"

## REFLECT ON THE MESSAGE

What can I do today?

# Notes

[1] Wiersbe, pp. 153-163

# Day 29

# What a School

### READ THE MANUSCRIPT

Ecclesiastes 12:9-12, "And moreover, because the preacher was wise, he still taught the people knowledge; yea, he gave good heed, and sought out, and set in order many proverbs. The preacher sought to find out acceptable words: and that which was written was upright, even words of truth. The words of the wise are as goads, and as nails fastened by the masters of assemblies, which are given from one shepherd. And further, by these, my son, be admonished: of making many books there is no end; and much study is a weariness of the flesh."

### REVIEW THE MATERIAL

Life is like school. You are constantly learning. You are passing or failing. Solomon was a student of life. Throughout Ecclesiastes, he is searching, experimenting, and trying to discover the meaning of life. Verse 9 confirms he was a wise man. He was a teacher. He was a scientist who approached life in an orderly fashion. Verse 10 records how careful he was to say or write the correct words. He sought to combine grace and truth with his words. Verse 11 says his words came from One Shepherd. I believe this speaks of inspiration, the process of how the Holy Spirit hovered over Solomon. Solomon wrote from his own personality but was moved by the Holy Spirit, so that today, when we read the Bible, we notice different styles from the different writers. Yet we can have confidence that what we read is from God. The Bible is the word of God. It is the inerrant, infallible, inspired word of God.

Solomon uses the terms "goads" and "nails" in Verse 11. Goads were used to prod people to pay attention and pursue truth. I wish ushers in our churches had some goads to prod people to pay attention. I am going to get some for our teachers at Jacksonville College to use in the classroom. Much failure in the schoolhouse and the house of life is students who do not pay attention.

Nails were something onto which students could hang what they learned. This is the teacher's task, to show the student how truth is to be applied. Facts without practical application will get lost. Every lesson should make sense. Often this does not happen and the student leaves the classroom and responds, "That did not make sense." A parishioner will leave the church house and say, "I did not get one thing out of that message."

Verse 12 reminds us we are to be lifelong learners. One should never graduate from learning. The mission statement of Jacksonville College states that Jacksonville College exists to provide a quality education from a Biblical worldview that challenges minds and transforms lives that results in servant leaders and (notice) lifelong learners.

In every subject of life, every issue, every problem, every book we read, every speech we hear, all should be tested against the word of God. There are many philosophies of man's ideas floating around. Test them against what God says.

Life is a school. Our textbook is the Bible and, as I tell my class, I am not the teacher, the Holy Spirit is the teacher. 1

## REMEMBER YOUR MAKER

O, Holy Spirit, I yield my mind and body to you. Teach me today.

## ROAR WITH MIRTH

A fisherman returned to shore with a giant marlin that was bigger and heavier than he. On the way to the cleaning shed, he ran into a second fisherman who had a stringer with a dozen small fish. The second fisherman looked at the marlin, turn to the first fisherman and said, "Only caught one, eh?"

## REFLECT ON THE MESSAGE

What is God trying to teach me today?

# Notes

[1] Wiersbe, p. 155-156

# Day 30

# What a Stewardship

## READ THE MANUSCRIPT

Ecclesiastes 12:13-14, "Let us hear the conclusion of the whole matter: Fear God, and keep his commandments: for this is the whole duty of man. For God shall bring every work into judgment, with every secret thing, whether it be good, or whether it be evil."

## REVIEW THE MATERIAL

Steward means manager. In life, a person will be more satisfied if they come to these conclusions:

1. God is the Creator and Owner of all. Psalms 24:1, "The earth is the Lord's and the fullness thereof; the world and they that dwell therein." God owns everything. That's why, if you will come to accept this, tithing and giving to the local church 10% of all you earn will not be hard. Many young believers resist tithing. But if you come to the place that you own nothing, it is all God's, then giving 10%, 15%, or 20%, will not be difficult. It is not your money, not your time, and not your

life. Salvation is to die to self and receive the new life with Jesus as your Lord. [1]

2. You are a steward. You are to manage what God has entrusted to you. Some people say, "I wish I had more money." How are you managing what God has entrusted to you? Too many people go through life wasting time, talent, and treasure (money) on their wants and desires. They end up in life dissatisfied. If we are to be good stewards, then Solomon shares in Ecclesiastes 12:13-14 what we must do:

- Fear God. This means we must respect God. We must believe He is creator. If we truly believe he is creator, then we will stand in awe and have reverence and respect. Warren Wiersbe quotes Oswald Chambers, "The remarkable thing about fearing God is that when you fear God, you fear nothing else; whereas, if you do not fear God, you fear everything else."[2]

- Fight to keep his commandments. I say fight because life is a struggle. In this life, our flesh will constantly be pulled away from God's word. Daily we will be tempted. It takes a concerted effort on our part to obey God.

- Final judgment. We all will stand before God in judgment one day. Lost people, who have rejected God, will stand before the Great White Throne of Judgment. Revelation 20 describes the event where lost people stand before God and every person who has rejected Jesus as Lord and Savior in this life, with their names not written in the book of life, will be cast into the lake of fire. Revelation 20:15, says, "and whosoever was not found written in the book of life was cast into the lake of fire." Every believer will be judged at the Bema Seat, the Judgment Seat of Christ. Only Christians will be at this judgment. So, this judgment is not to determine if you are saved or lost or going to heaven or hell. Here, a Christian's works will be judged. 2 Corinthians 5:10 says, "For we must all appear before the judgment seat of Christ; that every one may receive the things done in his body, according to that he hath done, whether it be good or bad." Have we been good stewards of all God has entrusted to us?

## REMEMBER OUR MAKER

God, help me to be a good steward today.

## ROAR WITH MIRTH

The nurse came into the office and said to the Doctor, "There's a man in the waiting room who thinks he's invisible. What should I tell him?" The Doctor said, "Tell him I can't see him today."

## REFLECT ON THE MESSAGE

Today I will seek God first and seek to manage carefully all He gives me.

# Notes

[1] Boss,master
[2] Wiersbe, p. 137

# Day 31

# Wise Summary

**READ THE MANUSCRIPT**

Ecclesiastes 12:13-14, "Let us hear the conclusion of the whole matter: Fear God, and keep his commandments: for this is the whole duty of man. For God shall bring every work into judgment, with every secret thing, whether it be good, or whether it be evil."

**REVIEW THE MATERIAL**

Ecclesiastes starts out with Solomon in search for meaning in life. Remember all the pursuits of Solomon to find purpose. He tried:

- Wisdom – 1:12-18
- Wit – 2:1-2
- Wine – 2:3
- Women – 2:7
- Wealth – 2:8-9

- Work – 2:10-26
- Worship – 2:24-26
- Watch (Time) – 3:1-11
- Wife – 4:9-12
- World of Politics – 4:1-3

After experimenting with all life has to give, Solomon concludes all is vanity. Vanity means empty, useless. Nothing in life can satisfy Solomon. So, the book concludes in 12:13, "Let us hear the conclusion of the whole matter: Fear God, and keep his commandments."

Solomon concluded that God is the only one to give purpose and joy to life. Stand back and observe people. It is sad to see people throw their lives away. I thank God that he gives jobs, purpose, and meaning to life.

## REMEMBER YOUR MAKER

God, thank you for life.

## ROAR WITH MIRTH

A young lady has sharp pains in her side. The doctor examines her and says, "You have acute appendicitis." The young lady says, "That's sweet, Doc, I'm glad you think my appendicitis is cute, but I came here to get medical help."

## REFLECT ON THE MESSAGE

I choose today to resist the allurements of this world and enjoy the life in Christ.

# Bibliography

Akin, Daniel, and Jonathan Akin, Christ-Centered Exposition. Exalting Jesus in Ecclesiastes. Nashville, Tennessee: B&H Publishing Group. 2016

Stedman, Ray C. Is This All There is to Life? Answers from Ecclesiastes. Grand Rapids, Michigan: Discovery House Publishers. 1999

Wiersbe, Warren W. Be Satisfied Old Testament Commentary Ecclesiastes. Colorado Springs: David C. Cook. 1990

Young, Ed. Been There Done That Now What? Nashville, Tennessee. B&H Publishing Group. 1994

All the **Roar with Mirth** entries come from my friend, Ed Hart. Ed is Director of Missions in New York. In his regular newsletter, Hart to Heart, he has a section, "Have you Heard This One?" These jokes come from his 2018-19 newsletters.

# About the Author

Dr. Mike Smith,
President, Jacksonville College in Jacksonville, Texas

Dr. Smith holds several academic degrees, including an Associate of Arts from Blinn College, a Bachelor of Arts from Baylor University, and a Master of Divinity and a Master of Religious Education from Southwestern Baptist Theological Seminary in Fort Worth. He has an earned doctorate from Luther Rice Seminary, as well as a Doctor of Ministry degree and a Doctor of Philosophy degree from Southern Seminary in Louisville, Kentucky.

Dr. Smith has taught courses as Adjunct Professor at the Baptist Missionary Association Theological Seminary in Jacksonville, and for Southwestern Baptist Theological Seminary in Fort Worth. He has served on the Jacksonville College Board of Visitors, and has also been a member of the Board of Trustees for the college.

Dr. Smith pastored churches for 17 years in Texas at Gatesville, Frost, Valley View, Edom, and Terrell. He has worked with the Home Mission Board of the Southern Baptist Convention as a church planter in Illinois, and has served as 2nd Vice Chairman of the International Mission Board for the SBC. From 1995 to 2008, Smith was Director of Missions of the Dogwood Trails Baptist Area in Jacksonville. Prior to that, he was Director of Missions at Double Mountain Baptist Area in Stamford, Texas for eight years. He served as Director of the Minister/Church Relations Department for the Southern Baptists of Texas Convention for three years before becoming president of Jacksonville College in 2011. He also teaches Old and New Testament Survey courses at Jacksonville College. He starts each class day with a devotional from Proverbs and prayer.

Mike Smith has been married to Susan Springer Smith for forty-two years. They have two children, Martha Elain Gardner and Lance Curtis Smith. They have five grandchildren, William, Emma, and Jacob Gardner, and Logan and Landon Smith. they also count as their children son-in-law, James Gardner and daughter-in-law, Ashley Smith.

His other books include:
- *Conflict: Causes and Cures.*
- *A Proverb A Day: Daily Wisdom For Living* (Available in English and Spanish)
- *The 5 W's of Every Old Testament Book*
- *Daily Beside The Still Waters: Devotions From Psalms*

The goal of Franklin Publishing is to enable Pastors, Evangelists, Missionaries, and Christian leaders and presenters to become published authors. Becoming a published author expands your influence and builds your ministry. You can write the book or sermon series which God has laid on your heart. We can walk that road with you.

www.FranklinPublishing.org

Come and visit our Facebook page and be sure to like and follow us to keep up with writing tips and new developments.

www.facebook.com/FranklinPublishing

www.ingramcontent.com/pod-product-compliance
Lightning Source LLC
LaVergne TN
LVHW051501070426
835507LV00022B/2871